TEACHING FOR A CHANGE

TEACHING FOR A CHANGE

A Transformational
Approach to Education

*Do not be conformed to this world, but be transformed by
the renewing of your mind, that you may prove what is
that good and acceptable and perfect will of God.*

ROMANS 12:2

Norman De Jong

P U B L I S H I N G
P.O. BOX 817 • PHILLIPSBURG • NEW JERSEY 08865-0817

Unless otherwise indicated, Scripture quotations are from The Holy Bible, New King James Version. Copyright © 1979, 1980, 1982, Thomas Nelson, Inc.

Scripture quotations marked (NIV) are from the HOLY BIBLE, NEW INTERNATIONAL VERSION®. NIV®. Copyright © 1973, 1978, 1984 by International Bible Society. Used by permission of Zondervan Publishing House. All rights reserved.

Scripture quotations marked (NASB) are from the New American Standard Bible. Copyright by the Lockman Foundation 1960, 1962, 1963, 1968, 1971, 1973, 1975, 1977.

Page design by Tobias Design
Typesetting by Michelle Feaster

Printed in the United States of America

Library of Congress Cataloging-in-Publication Data

De Jong, Norman.
    Teaching for a change : a transformational approach to education / Norman De Jong.
        p.   cm.
    Includes bibliographical references and index.
    ISBN 0-87552-176-2 (pbk.)
    1. Moral education—United States. 2. Christian ethics—Study and teaching—United States. 3. Education—Aims and objectives—United States.
I. Title.

LC311.D42 2001
370.11'4'0973—dc21

00-066929

To

Craig, Nathan, Samantha,
Nick, Ian, Bradley, Ana, Gracie,
Holly, Elijah, Jenna, Cameron,

twelve of the most wonderful
grandchildren a person could ever have.
May all of you learn what it means to be
transformed into the mind of Christ.

Contents

Acknowledgments

Finding a way to express appreciation for all those who have contributed to the formation of this book is a difficult chore. Over the years that these ideas have been forming, numerous people have given me insights, challenged my formulations, and honed my perspectives. Some of them were friendly, helping me in positive ways. Others were adversarial, challenging me on fundamental issues. Possessing a love for Christian education, with a God-centered focus, brought me into conflict with many delightful proponents of subject-centered schools. To begin to name any of those folks would be an exercise in planned omissions, with probable offense to all.

There is one group of persons, though, who deserve special mention. These are the members of Covenant Presbyterian Church of Orland Park, Illinois. Knowing my love for Christian education, they gave me permission to take an early retirement from their ministry so that I might devote my time to writing this manuscript. Since they too have a long-term commitment to the cause, they probably hoped for some benefit to their own thinking and that of their children. It is my prayer that many of them might find inspiration and wisdom in these pages. To all of them, a fond and sincere "thank you" for the early release from my ministerial responsibilities.

A second group of individuals who deserve special recognition are the twelve grandchildren to whom this book is dedicated. As I have had the privilege of watching them grow from newborn infants into budding teenagers, they have afforded me numerous examples of the basic biblical truths that grace these pages. Lovable and sweet as they are, they still confirm the truths of total depravity and original sin. At the same time, they have modeled for me what it means to be born in the image of God, putting on display remarkable gifts of grace, including that of consciences that serve as a brake on our human tendencies. Their names, you will note, also appear occasionally throughout this book, giving me some delightful focal points as I tell a true story or sketch an important concept.

The parents of those twelve deserve special mention, for they have offered many opportunities to discuss the natural traits that those little saints displayed. To Greg and Kathy, to Brian and DeLou, and to Mark and Amy, thank you for blessing us with such wonderful children whom you are striving to nurture in the fear and knowledge of God. Without you, they would not have graced our lives.

Particular individuals who gave specific help on various occasions include my wife, Wilma, who once again read every page and gave me frequent suggestions for improvement. A second person is my son Brian, who did important research assignments for me, simply because I knew he loved the cause and could provide quick, solid answers to sticky questions. A third person who gave me much inspiration was none other than Barbara Lerch of P&R Publishing. Her enthusiastic endorsement of the early chapters served as a wonderful spur for me to keep on writing, to develop the entire manuscript, and to bring it to this stage.

There are probably many others who deserve mention in this space, but their credits will probably have to wait until they get to glory, where justice reigns supreme.

Introduction

On Tuesday, April 20, 1999, Littleton, Colorado, became etched on the pages of American history. With chilling precision and boiling hatred, two teenage boys entered Columbine High School and began killing their classmates in a manner and number never before experienced by schools in this country. Fueled by Nazi ideology, satanic religion, and Goth culture, these two boys systematically killed twelve classmates and one teacher, seriously injured sixteen other people, took their own lives, and terrified a nation. Within hours, people watched their television and computer screens or listened to their radios as the grisly scene became known to millions around the world.

The scene, once unthinkable, is no longer unusual. We have heard of similar shootings in places like Pearl, Mississippi; Paducah, Kentucky; Jonesboro, Arkansas; Springfield, Oregon; Santee, California. The numbers of dead and wounded at such places may not equal those in Littleton, but that is small consolation. Neither is such violence unique to schools, for post offices and office buildings are equally the targets of mad terrorists.

What makes the school shootings so alarming is that the atrocities are meticulously carried out by juveniles whose hatred for their fellow students has been fueled by rock culture, television, and the free fare on the Internet. Kids who are not old enough to drive an automobile are adept at making pipe bombs and spouting satanic verses. Kids who have not learned how to love are proficient at hatred. Kids who have not learned to honor their fathers and mothers have come to idolize the sex and drug symbols of mass culture. Kids who would not willingly put a nickel in a church collection plate are eager to fork over $29.50 for a rock concert ticket and another $15.00 for a CD by their favorite purveyor of violence and sex.

What is wrong? Why do kids love brutality? What could possibly drive two seemingly normal kids to engage in unspeakable slaughter of classmates and teachers?

The answers, offered by those carefully selected to represent the wishes of the media, usually sniff at the symptoms and seldom examine the causes. Expressing a sympathetic consternation at the behaviors and the resultant carnage, most of these experts will fail to admit that America and the West have become increasingly pagan, with even the evangelical Christian community leapfrogging over itself to imitate the world around it. The difference between the world and the church at times like these hardly seems distinguishable. At bottom, both embrace the tenets of secular humanism, with neither having a grasp of the fundamental truths that permeate Scripture and address the questions that need to be asked.

One example of misdirected analysis is the notion that kids who carry guns to school have learned hatred. If that is true, whoever must have taught them to hate is really to blame. The poor youngster, maniacal in his meticulous planning, is simply carrying through on those teachings. He or she, like all of the rest of us, is to be pitied as a victim, a product of this culture.

The premise beneath that analysis is fatally flawed. We don't become evil. We are born that way. We don't learn hatred. We are naturally inclined in that direction from birth. We are not victims of our culture, even though we may be powerfully influenced by it. We are responsible agents, created in the image of God but fallen in the line of Adam and Eve.

But like that of our first parents, our first response to our own fallenness is fear and blameshifting. The national dialogue following the Columbine tragedy reminded me of the reaction to the Russians' successful launching of Sputnik in 1957. Suddenly, in panic, the nation arose to address the issue and to face its worst fears. Then as now, everyone from the president to governors to legislators to preachers and everyone else in between began the process of assessing blame and pointing fingers of accusation.

One of the most clear-sighted and intelligent responses to the Colorado massacre came from an editorial in *World* magazine, in which Joel Belz opined, "A quarter century ago, you worried about whether your kids would be safe on the icy roads to school. Now you worry about whether they'll be safe once they get to school. That evidences a sobering transition for our society—and the marks of the transition are all around us. We are digging in. We're all shifting from offense to defense."[1]

There is tremendous evidence of a defensive posturing on behalf of our nation's schools, but that will not solve the problems we face at this juncture in our history. According to the Statistical Abstract of the United States, in 1996 there were 1.3 million reported incidents in our nation's schools, with 255,000 of them classified as serious, involving murders, suicides, and rapes.[2] The problem has obviously been widespread, but we needed the sledgehammer of Littleton to get our national attention. Like Missouri mules, we needed to be hit hard on the head before we awoke to the challenge.

We as Christians have more than defensive explanations of why such behavior is becoming commonplace. As persons who have rich biblical insights into the causes of aberrant human behavior, we can offer truthful explanations of why evil rises to the surface and why such seemingly irrational actions become customary. We also have, or at least ought to have, positive, offensive strategies that will address the issues of the human heart at its core. We, of all people, ought to have a philosophy of education that not only will prevent such violent expressions of hatred but will produce the peaceable fruits of righteousness.

This book has been in the planning stages for at least two years. The tragedy in Littleton did not motivate it or shape it. As a successor to *Education in the Truth*, which had run its course after five editions, this manuscript was intended to give a fresh look at the basic truths that ought to mold our educational endeavors. But there was no urgency. At least there was none until the events at Columbine High School shook our national confidence to the core and spawned hundreds of copycat, can-you-top-this plans by would-be high school assassins all across the land. Suddenly there was urgency to the writing.

There is a fundamental need for a biblical, Christian philosophy of education for a land that is becoming more and more secular and for a people who are becoming more and more pagan. Our children are being reared in a culture where abortion, pornography, adultery, promiscuous sex, greed, gambling, and homosexuality are accepted as alternative lifestyles and legalized behaviors subject to no civil penalty. Although there are occasional, spasmodic outbursts of religious fervor, especially after such tragedies as those experienced in Oklahoma City and Littleton, secular humanism remains the only officially established religion in the land. Humanism, however, is hopelessly bankrupt, with no enduring foundation and no hope except for more of the sadness already experienced.

But there is another side to this rash of schoolhouse bombings and shootings that needs our attention. For more than a year the two boys who caused the Columbine catastrophe were part of a well-known and easily recognized gang on campus called the Trenchcoat Mafia. Although there were as many as fifteen known members whose clothing and personal styles clearly signaled their love for both Satan and Hitler, no one seemed to care. Parents seemed to pay no attention to what these young men were doing in their bedrooms or how they dressed when they left for school. Classmates who knew of their intense hatred for various campus groups and who knew of their penchant for high-powered guns and bombs religiously observed the teenagers' eleventh commandment: Thou shalt not squeal. Teachers and administrators apparently refused to confront them, probably for fear of reprisal. Why didn't anyone care enough to say, "Stop it! No more of that!"?

The answer, I suspect, is because of a warped, bankrupt philosophy of education that has been promulgated by all the universities and wannabe universities of the land. For huge segments of our population, education is nothing more than the imparting of neutral knowledge and job skills sufficient to fill one's economic needs. For others, education is essentially nothing more than adjustment to a culture of relativism, with collective humanity the only determiner of what is acceptable behavior. In such a mindset, self-esteem is the primary product of good pedagogy, with safe sex not far behind. Both positions are intellectual, psychological, and moral wastelands. Both lead, almost inevitably, to a fear of the consumer, to a genuine fear of the kids we are supposed to educate. With no abiding values or eternal truths on which to cling, the driving reason for a continuing career in the classroom is the security of a contract and the increasingly satisfactory paycheck.

The level of harassment to which I will allude in "A Tale of Two Towns" is almost frivolous when compared with the threats and violence experienced in America's schools during the last decade. More than forty years ago, smashing rotten eggs against a teacher's house or car was enough to intimidate many idealistic young pedagogues or drive them out of the profession. Two young men who began their careers in the same school in the same year as I did hung up the chalk after one nine-month stint in front of a class. They didn't need any harassment.

One of the things that kept me going was the appearance at my classroom door of a young soldier with a confession that stirred my heart and soul. It was not new to me, for I had said virtually the same thing to my dad five years before. After resisting my father's teachings for years, I finally came to realize that he was right and I was wrong. Then, at a point of private and personal confession, I began to experience the joy of learning to live according to the truth. There was truth, and the grasp of it brought peace, contentment, satisfaction, and wondrous rewards. I intuitively knew that such could happen when I tried to transmit the truths of the ages to the next generation. I too knew that teaching could bring a tremendous sense of satisfaction. A young man named Sammy would soon teach me that important lesson.

——1 Understanding the Dilemma

A Tale of Two Towns

It was 6:30 A.M. when everything seemed to happen. Wilm, my wife of less than one year, burst into the apartment. With a look of shock and utter dismay on her face, she cried out, "The car is covered with rotten eggs! It has eggs all over it! They're smashed against the windows, on the trunk, everywhere!" I raced outside with her and went into the detached garage that came with our upstairs apartment. Just as she had said, our 1951 maroon Chevy sedan was covered with rotten eggs, obviously not laid by some chickens roosting in the rafters overhead but thrown there by some enterprising person or persons who had little chance of missing at the short range afforded by a double-stall garage with access off the back alley.

Wilm was scheduled to work that day at the Pipestone Hospital, twenty miles down the road, and was due on the floor at seven. A quick exam under the hood of our auto convinced me that she could never make that, even if she drove down the road under a blanket of eggshells. The culprits, whoever they might be, had obviously been into the engine compartment as well, for every wiring harness was pulled from its mooring and lay in a bundle on top of the engine block. This car would not run until a mechanic had time to put it all back together.

My mind was racing. Who could have done this? Who could be so mean and vicious as to do so much damage to my auto and my ego? We had been in this little southwestern Minnesota town for slightly over six weeks. Having earned an M.A. in recent American history at the University of Iowa in August, I had accepted my first teaching contract at Southwest Minnesota Christian High School and confronted my first class the Tuesday after Labor Day. Those first days I was full of jitters and nervous energy, but the classes had gone well, and I was already becoming acquainted with the seven groups of high schoolers to whom I was assigned. Most of them were farm-raised and used to hard work, with one or two coming to school with fresh cow manure still clinging to their shoes. The odor was not so pleasant, but the attitudes were conducive to serious study. At least they gave that impression during the first six weeks.

The day before, in my 12 A and 12 B English literature classes, I had returned the first tests that I had constructed. Most of the students had done well, with a sizable dose of A's and B's to balance out the C's and D's. There were only two failing grades, both in the B section. Reggie and Sammy had not shown much joy when I handed their tests back, since the grade distribution chart I had put on the board clearly indicated that they were the only ones to have failed the first English exam.

Standing there in the garage, looking at my maroon sedan now covered with yellow and greenish-white slime, my thoughts turned immediately to those two. Who else could have so much hatred toward me so early in my career? I took Wilm back to the house and had her call the hospital to tell them that she would not be able to come in that day. Then I made two short telephone calls.

Knowing Sammy's father's name, I dialed the farm phone and waited a few rings for someone to pick it up. It was now about 6:45. A middle-aged man said hello, to which I responded, "Let me speak to Sammy."

"Sammy is still in bed," the man replied. "Who is calling?"

"Let me speak to Sammy."

"Okay, I'll get him up. You'll have to wait a minute."

Within a few minutes, Sammy came to the phone and said, "Hello."

"I'll give you exactly one half hour to get over here and clean up my car. If you don't, I'll have the sheriff come by and pick you up." Without giving direction and without identifying myself in any way, I hung up.

I immediately looked up Reggie's phone number and repeated

the process with him. He asked who was calling, but I emphasized the expected arrival time of 7:30, when he should be on my doorstep. I then hung up, grabbed some cereal, and waited.

Promptly at 7:30, the doorbell rang. I went down the stairs, there to find Sammy and Reggie waiting. I asked them what they were doing at my door at such an early hour on a school day, to which they replied, "You called, didn't you?" They realized that they had convicted themselves. I obviously had the culprits who had visited my garage during the previous evening.

I gave them a series of ultimatums: The car was to be washed, cleaned thoroughly, and polished. All of the wiring was to be reattached so that it ran as smoothly as new, even if that meant having the car towed to a garage. And they were to pay my wife twenty-five dollars for lost wages. All the penalties had to be met before nightfall, or else the sheriff would still be called. When I got to school an hour later, I reported my problems to the principal, who concurred with my judgments and promised to help in my dealings with the two boys.

With some bitter complaining about the twenty-five-dollar payment, Sammy and Reggie met the requirements and got an unexcused absence for the classes they missed that morning. Their attitudes were not great demonstrations of sweetness and cooperation, but we got through that year with some tough moments of confrontation and finally got to commencement, with both Sammy and Reggie earning enough credits for graduation.

That summer Sammy went off to join the army. Reggie went to work for a local garage, pumping gas and doing simple mechanical work. The second year of teaching proved to be much easier than the first. I had the confidence of having survived the crucial first year in the classroom. Two-thirds of the faculty who had begun their careers the same time I had did not return, so I felt somewhat successful but still overworked.

One day in late September I was ensconced behind the closed door of my classroom castle when I heard a faint knock. Pausing in the middle of a mundane explanation of some point in English grammar, I walked to the door and was greeted with a humble, "Excuse me, but can I talk to you for a minute?"

There, decked out in his military uniform, stood Sammy. "Sir, can I talk with you for just a minute? I want to apologize for all the trouble I caused you last year. I am sorry for what I did and for my terrible attitude. I've learned a lot during the last year, and I want to thank you for everything you did for me."

Tears welled up in my eyes. I couldn't say anything at first but finally blurted out, "Thank you." I was so glad he had come back, so grateful for those few words of gratitude and the implied compliments that went with it. With new vigor and excitement, I went back into my classroom, facing a bunch of sometimes incorrigible seniors who saw no need for diagramming sentences or memorizing dates of English history. Teaching would always be rewarding, as long as there were Sammies around.

After a second year in Edgerton, which was full of persistent challenges and increasing rewards, Wilm and I moved to another small town, in western Montana. A former high school principal had recommended me for the daunting task of elementary administrator, a job for which I was ill prepared but courageous enough to accept. The area was beautiful, the trout fishing fabulous, and the people hospitable. Three years there were delightful, with blessings too numerous to mention. But there were also the inevitable challenges.

From day one, there were three boys, one in the seventh grade and two in the sixth, who found innumerable ways to harass their teachers. True to form, their teachers came to the office with their complaints and their pleas for support. I did the best I could, giving encouragement and helpful hints as to how to control and redirect these boys' behavior. One day, in a seemingly deliberate show of defiance, one of the boys came to school driving the family car, parking it conspicuously in line with my office window. Richie was in the seventh grade and had barely passed his thirteenth birthday. His parents lived almost directly across the street from the school parking lot, so there was no need for transportation, let alone for him to be driving. He had to pull himself up in the driver's seat to look out the windshield. Slamming the door shut, he strode toward the entrance where I could not avoid him and proceeded toward his class.

Not bothering to confront this perennial troublemaker, I let him go by and called his home instead. Obviously this act of defiance was done with parental knowledge and probably with fatherly encouragement. Dad had a reputation, well earned, of having one of the shortest fuses in town, with a temper that could blow at the slightest provocation. It wasn't long before Rich Senior pulled up in the parking lot and headed for the main entrance. Coming directly into my office without bothering to knock, he asked if I had a problem with his son taking the car to school. With his huge, muscular frame not three feet from where I was sitting, he threatened to "knock my block off" if I stood up. Not wishing to have my brain rattled or my sinuses cleared, I remained sitting and prayed for calmness and composure. The Lord heard my prayer and helped me through another one of those unpleasant confrontations that administrators often have to endure.

When I reported this incident to our board of directors their advice was for me to avoid ever meeting this man or any of his close friends in a place where protection was scarce, for he truly was capable of harming me or any of the teachers who would dare to challenge him.

Not surprisingly, this young fellow and the two other tormentors caused the teachers and myself no end of harassment in the years ahead. Trying every psychological trick that our collective heads could conjure up, we finally resigned ourselves to enduring the juvenile persecution that these untamed brats could muster, short of being incarcerated.

The final humiliation that I had to endure occurred more than three years later, after my family and I had moved back to the Midwest. Longing for a chance to renew relationships with all the wonderful people who had become our lifelong friends, as well as another chance to snare some beautiful rainbows out of their plentiful streams, we returned to the wonders of Montana for some well-earned vacation. On our final day in Churchill, as I began to pack the car, I noticed that two of the tires had been slashed and would need to be replaced. Was this a random act of violence by someone needing to test the mettle of his Swiss army knife? Or was this a planned attack by those who had found new ways to demonstrate their hatred, smoldering after years of absence? I suspected the latter, but I had no proof and could expect no cooperation from any of the parents, so we replaced the tires and headed for home.

As we traveled across the high ranges of Montana and Wyoming, it became evident that our troubles were not over. Still basking in the warm reception of the majority of wonderful families there but also smarting from the rejection of boys who knew only hatred, we tried to get home in a most direct route. That was not to be. Periodically, with no warning, the car would sputter, die, and lurch to a stop. After we'd scratched our heads, looked under the hood, and cautiously vented our frustration, the car would start again and allow us to travel for unpredictable distances. We got home, after numerous stops at garages along the way, but with the problem unresolved. Months later, in desperation, we sold the car and bought another.

Not long after, the new owner reported that he had found the problem. Removing the gas tank, he had found inside it a number of gas-soaked crab apples, small enough to fit through the opening and large enough to seal off the gas line. The boys whose parents could never admit their wrongs had struck once again.

More than thirty years later, at a gathering of church leaders, I encountered one of their classmates. Now an elder in a solidly biblical church, this godly man reported what had happened to Richie and his two friends in the years since we had moved away. Throughout their high school years, all three had been in repeated trouble and caused others as much grief as they had directed at me. All three had gotten into trouble with law enforcement agencies and had spent time in jail for a variety of offenses. Living in defiance of God's law, their lives had been cursed and their reputations ruined. Although they had mocked their Creator, He was true to His promises: "If you obey Me, I will bless you, but if you do not obey, I will curse you." Too stubborn to listen, they have reaped their reward, full of bitterness, hatred, and pain.

In Search of a Reason

The majority of young children and teenagers with whom I worked in Montana were not like Richie and his buddies. Quite the contrary, they were delightful, honest, and hard-working kids, not ever totally angelic and not ever totally devilish, but always curious. Their honesty came in their questions: "Why must we study grammar? Why must we study such silly poetry as Shelley's 'Sonnets' or Longfellow's

'Evangeline'? Why should we know the scientific names for the different plants? Why should we learn the dates of the American Revolution? Why should we have to study algebraic formulas? Why should we have to . . . ?"

Their questions were not nasty. They were being honest and wanted relevant answers. Where does a teacher find cogent answers to such basic questions?

Maybe we ought to ask students what they would like to study. Maybe we ought to consult the writings of the great John Dewey to find out what our educational program should look like. Maybe we ought to look carefully at the world in which students live and in which the majority assume they will continue to reside, and find there the kinds of learning relevant to their lives.

As a young educator, maybe I could find the answers in the curriculum required of superintendent candidates at Montana State University, where I enrolled for summer school programs, all with the hope of earning the credentials necessary to move to the top of the school administration circuit. Maybe the courses in public relations, in finance, in school record keeping, in staff management, in curriculum design, or in school law would give me the kinds of reasons that would impress these inquisitive kids. Certainly a course in curriculum construction for cultural consensus would provide the clues.

Maybe I could find the answers in the annals of school law, for here was a fascinating field, full of fact and fiction. In the legal history of the United States, especially as it pertains to the function and form of the educational establishment, might be the kinds of reasons for studying algebra, ancient history, English grammar, Latin, or spelling. All of my students' farm jobs, which they already did with high levels of proficiency, could be accomplished without any of those subjects.

Maybe I could find an answer in the annual reports of Horace Mann, who pushed his agenda of a Christless Christianity in the state of Massachusetts during the 1840s and thus foisted on an unsuspecting nation the theology of the Unitarian establishment. Maybe the secular public schools he helped to establish had the answers. Maybe Dewey or Plato or Aristotle or Immanuel Kant would provide the reasons for setting up schools and then demanding, against their repeated wishes, that kids attend. Maybe a smorgasbord of reasons advanced by philosophers down through the ages would give students ample incentive.

The persistent queries of these young people forced me to change the direction of my graduate studies. No longer finding much comfort in the mundane courses of educational administration, I pursued a degree in educational philosophy. I was nagged by the kids' legitimate desires to have a valid reason for studying the curriculum we thrust in front of them. I needed answers for myself so that I could defend what I and some of their parents insisted was good for them. Not nearly all of their fathers and mothers were on the same page, but most were not willing or ready to defy the laws of the land. The state, after all, required of every able-bodied youngster a specified number of high school credits and a presence in some school for a minimum number of days, at least until their sixteenth birthday. Should they not cooperate, we always had the threat of taking away their activity privileges or of an after-school detention. We could take them off the basketball team or the baseball team or the track squad. What more compelling reason did we need?

Judging from recent test results, a much more compelling reason is needed today.

The Dilemma Educators Face

Almost every year, in states all across the country, debates rage about the awful condition of our nation's public schools. For years, the newspapers and popular media have been trumpeting the drop in achievement test scores. Math proficiency, from grade three through grade twelve, is at an all-time low. Reading scores also seem to be steadily dropping every year, with an occasional blip on the chart creating ecstasy in the hearts of some educators. More and more people are classified as nonreaders, even though they have graduated from the eighth grade. *Crisis in the Classroom* becomes a best seller. *Why Johnny Can't Read* stirs a national debate. Personnel managers decry the fact that they cannot hire enough qualified workers because the typical high school graduate lacks the basic skills. In widespread response, families set up home schools, thus stirring another whirlwind of debate. Mothers give up outside employment in order to take over the role of teacher. The *Chicago Tribune* publishes its assessment under the title "Chicago Schools: Worst in America" (1988). When, ten years later, under an astute mayor and a courageous superintendent, those same schools are trumpeted at the national governors' conference as having vastly improved, every other governor's question is What went right?

The search for solutions to a cacophony of complaints goes on and on. With each act of senseless vandalism and every threat of violence, the questions surface again. Is something dreadfully wrong with the educational system? What are we doing to deserve this awful mess? With students at risk not only academically but also physically, something must be done to fix the problem. To complain about the deficiency is not enough. Parent and community meetings are organized to combat the problem, sometimes surreptitiously in activists' kitchens. School board meetings become webs of political intrigue and shouting matches among boisterous belligerents. With increasing frequency, teachers' unions organize rallies on state capitol steps, hoping to persuade their legislators to channel more money into their trough. State and national politicians jump into the fray, hoping to say the right words at the right moment, thereby reaping potential votes for the next election.

The latest solution, loudly debated on both sides, is the explosive suggestion of vouchers. Instead of funding only the state's public schools, let children and their parents receive a voucher for any school—public, parochial, or private. Look at how effective they have been in both Milwaukee and in Cleveland, say the proponents. As was done with the GI bill in earlier times, let the recipient decide which school is best. Besides, it is argued, increased competition can only improve the public schools of the land. All children will thus benefit.

The person who lacks historical perspective might get caught up in the frenzied criticism of the moment and conclude that the entire system will disintegrate within a decade. Such mournful doom saying has been heard numerous times during my lifespan and tempered my responses. Historians, though, will look at the scene quite differently. Not willing to declare that history is cyclical in character, they do see patterns clearly developing. As the trends are analyzed over a period of time, a pendulum effect becomes apparent. For eight, twelve, or even fifteen years there will be a chorus of demands to strengthen the academic subjects. Those who hold center stage have a rather common complaint that the problem lies with the poor instruction in the academic subjects. The reason that math and reading scores go down is because the needs of the academicians have been ignored. To solve the problem will require more devotion to reading, arithmetic, English, history, and science. The problem, these folks assert, is that none of these subjects has been effectively and consistently taught. Increase the requirements, if necessary, by raising the minimum state standards, and the problem will quickly disappear. Schools are, after all, academic institutions. Schools are subject-centered.

Not so, chime in the critics. The problem is the reverse, swinging the pendulum in the opposite direction. These revisionists are ready to claim that we have failed the system because we have put too much emphasis on the academics. What needs our attention are the students. At the core of the educational process are children, kids, if you will. Our problems and failures have developed because we have not paid enough attention to their needs. If we realize how many of them come from broken homes, how many are latchkey kids, and how many arrive at their classroom door without breakfast, then we would be on the road to improvement. What we need are more hot meals served before school and more compassionate classroom teachers. The school is, after all is said and done, a place where real people with real needs gather. The school is, or at least ought to be, child-centered.

The national debate goes back and forth. The school is subject-centered and needs academic solutions. No, the school is child-centered and needs personal solutions. Not true, the reason Johnny can't read is because we haven't taught phonics. Nonsense! The reason Johnny can't read is because he doesn't have adequate heat in his bedroom and because his father is never home. Johnny can't read because his real needs have not been met and because nobody cares about him as a person.

Which side is right? Is the school best defined as an academic institution? Is the subject at the center of its continued existence and gradual improvement? Or is attention to the needs of the student the focal point where eventual success can be found? Is the school in its essence a place where people gather? Is the school essentially child-centered?

Table 1 illustrates this secular educational dilemma. Educators and wannabe teachers are confronted with this maddening choice, compelled to choose between the student and the academic subject. For many, the choice directs them to either the elementary or the secondary level. For the college student, wanting to become a certified teacher, the dilemma results in choosing either a major in elementary education or a major in history or English or math. The dilemma is real, with perennial pulling power in both directions. As you examine the table, picture that pendulum swinging from one side to the other in almost every decade. Where do you stand?

Table 1. The Secular Educational Dilemma

THE SUBJECT-CENTERED MODEL	THE CHILD-CENTERED MODEL
PRIMARY CHARACTERISTICS	PRIMARY CHARACTERISTICS
traditional subject divisions	child welfare is prime concern
letter grades and Carnegie units	mastery learning, no time concerns
academic mastery for job skills	outcome-based education
strong local control	strong state and federal control
morality without religion	democratic values emphasized
education is primarily intellectual	accepts Rousseau's model
rugged individualism	cooperative learning
PRIMARY OBJECTIVES OR GOALS	PRIMARY OBJECTIVES OR GOALS
mastery of facts	good self-image
preparation for job skills	happy, well-adjusted person
development of a common culture	multicultural acceptance
accumulate much knowledge	enhance self-esteem
aim for material success	toleration for others
professional careers	vocational employment

At the risk of losing friends and supporters from both sides of this debate, I will propose that both sides are emphatically wrong. Those who are cognizant of the weight of words will immediately clue in to the description that this is a secular educational dilemma. Christians should immediately realize that the import of secularism is to omit a place for God. The vast majority of educators, at all levels, do not include God in their educational equation. They are not atheists. They do not deny God's existence. But they have never been taught to think that God is an integral part of the education process.

By ignoring God, they choose either to put the child at the center or to put the academic subject at the center. For them, there are only three essential elements: the teacher, the student, and the subject. At their worst, God is only a figment of man's imagination. At best, God is a loving grandfather, kind and gentle to all persons but active only on Sunday mornings. God is the author of salvation for repentant sinners, but He is not involved in daily activities at the local school. God is integral to salvation, but He is irrelevant to learning how to read, write, or multiply. The Supreme Court of the United States has ruled His active presence as impermissible at any public school in the land. In a land where secular humanism has become the only established religion—the only one worthy of public funding—there is no place for God-centered education.

Even many well-intentioned Christians have fallen for this secular argument. Faced with a dilemma of humanist making, many devout conservatives have opted for the subject-centered approach to schooling. One seeming example is the response of noted conservative columnist Cal Thomas to the child-centered approach. He observes,

> Author Berit Kjos, in her 1995 book *Brave New Schools*, exposes the game plan of contemporary educators. She quotes Professor Benjamin Bloom, known as the father of outcome-based education, as saying: "The purpose of education and the schools is to change the thoughts, feelings, and actions of students." No, it isn't. It's to teach basic facts and truths.[1]

With disturbing frequency, both Roman Catholics and Protestants omit God from their descriptions of the educational process. If we are not careful, we can become numbed by the prevailing secular philosophy and forget that God demands the central place. The Creator of the human race does not want any of His creatures, either individually or collectively, to occupy the center stage. The Source of all knowledge and wisdom, who gives insight and understanding to all men liberally, does not want that knowledge to be idolized and to take His rightful place. This God, after all, describes Himself repeatedly as a "jealous God, visiting the iniquity of the fathers on the children" (Deut. 5:9 NASB) whenever His people threaten to worship any substitute or any one of His creations. When Moses questions the character of his Father, God directly replies, "You shall not worship any other god, for the LORD, whose name is Jealous, is a jealous God" (Ex. 34:14 NASB).[2]

The solution to this secular educational dilemma is simple, for there is no dilemma for the discerning Christian. There is no choice to be made, for God is central; both students and subjects are essential to the total process, but neither one is central. There must be a knowledge of and concern for the student, because education without a recipient is nothing more than hot air in a vacuum. There must be a fundamental and truthful grasp of the knowledge to be employed, for truth is essential to sound instruction. A teacher who does not know his or her subject is a tragedy, an employee to be evicted. But a teacher with all the academic credentials in the world, a person who does not understand and love the recipients of that instruction, is equally a tragedy. Good schools, in order to merit any approval, need to have in their philosophies a prominent place for both the child and the subject matter, as well as for the teachers.

How then do we solve the secular educational dilemma? Table 2 shows a third model, one that neglects neither the child nor content, but builds on the true center of education. The child-centered advocates are fundamentally flawed, but so are the subject-centered ones. Both sides in this national, recurring debate need to change their focus. Both sides need to become God-centered.

Table 2. Solving the Secular Educational Dilemma

SUBJECT-CENTERED MODEL	GOD-CENTERED MODEL	CHILD-CENTERED MODEL
PRIMARY CHARACTERISTICS	PRIMARY CHARACTERISTICS	PRIMARY CHARACTERISTICS
traditional subject divisions	integration of faith and learning	child welfare is primary concern
letter grades and Carnegie units	all knowledge comes from God	mastery learning, no time concerns
academic mastery for job skills	use all talents for God's glory	outcome-based education
strong local control	strong parental control	strong state and federal control
morality without religion	biblical religion	democratic values emphasized
education is primarily intellectual	well-formulated philosophy	accepts Rousseau's model
rugged individualism		cooperative learning
PRIMARY OBJECTIVES OR GOALS	PRIMARY OBJECTIVES OR GOALS	PRIMARY OBJECTIVES OR GOALS
mastery of facts	knowledge of God's Word	good self-image
preparation for job skills	service to the kingdom and others	happy, well-adjusted person
development of a common culture	attempts to transform culture	multicultural acceptance
accumulate much knowledge	discern between truth and falsehood	enhance self-esteem
aim for material success	prepare for obedient, loving lives	toleration for others
professional careers	promote the unity of Christ's body	vocational employment
	all thoughts captive to Christ	
	attempts to transform persons	

—2 Do We Dare Talk Philosophy?

Whenever we encounter some sort of crisis involving our schools, there is a renewed interest in philosophy. It happened in 1957, when Russia demonstrated its space superiority by sending the Sputnik satellite into orbit. It happened again during the 1960s, in response to the Vietnam war and the widespread student rebellions that helped bring that war to a conclusion. It happened during the 1980s, when academic achievement scores seemed to plummet on a national scale. It happened in the late 1990s, as Americans everywhere recoiled in fear from the senseless shootings that plagued our schools.

Guns and bombs are excuses for fear. But so is philosophy. Philosophy sounds so imposing, so threatening to the average classroom teacher, to the farmer, to the small business owner, and to board-of-education members. Philosophy is for people with their heads in the clouds who possess no earthly skills. Philosophy is of no practical value. It is abstract theorizing for people who teach in esoteric departments at state universities.

Such is the common perception, but the common perception is dreadfully wrong. Philosophy, when philosophically pulled apart, is composed of two words: *phile*, meaning "love," and *sophia*, meaning "wisdom." Philosophy is the love of wisdom. To be philosophical is to love wisdom and to despise foolishness. To be a philosopher is to be the kind of person who loves wisdom and who wants to see wisdom practiced.

Every person ought to be a philosopher. Every teacher ought to be a philosopher. Every board member ought to be a philosopher. Before too many objections are raised, we need to lay down some clearly understood qualifiers. There are professional philosophers, and there are amateur philosophers. The professional, as in any kind of endeavor, is one who is so competent and so proficient in the field that others will pay him or her[1] for doing work for them. Someone who intensely concentrates his efforts on understanding and articulating the collected wisdom pertaining to education will be hired by a college or a university to teach courses in the philosophy of education. He is then a professional. The classroom teacher, the precocious student, or the studious parent who reflectively analyzes what needs to occur in the educational process is also a philosopher, but only an amateur. No one pays him for his thinking and his speaking, but that does not stop him from doing either. That clear distinction between professional and amateur is most apparent in the world of sports, where countless men and women excel in any given sport, but no one pays them to play the sport for the sake of entertaining others.

All teachers ought to be philosophers and ought to take courses in that subject so as to enhance their insights and avoid the pitfalls of conventional practice. Every teacher ought to love wisdom and ought to model wise behavior, for students always learn by example and by imitation. All principals, superintendents, and curriculum coordinators ought also to see themselves as philosophers, for they too should love wisdom and despise foolishness.

To be a philosopher suggests other qualities, too. To love wisdom implies that there is a definition of wisdom that must be followed. Wisdom implies knowledge of what is true and how that truth can be distinguished from what is false or foolish. Wisdom also connotes the willingness to follow the truth, even when the consequences might cause some discomfort or potential harm. A wonderful old adage tells us that "honesty is the best policy." To be completely honest in every situation may cause short-term consequences that are less than pleasant, but in the long run complete honesty is the wisest course of action. When an employer wants you to propagate a popular falsehood, such as the lie of theistic evolution, your refusal to do so might cost you your job. When a supervisor wants you to doctor a report to minimize political fallout, your complicity in his schemes might warrant you a promotion, but it will never bring you peace of mind.

Philosophy is always a pursuit of the truth and demands allegiance to it. Foolishness is a pursuit of falsehood, with its attendant curses and consequences. Many who claim to be philosophers, including some of the most famous names associated with that area of academic expertise, are fools, for they suppress the truth in their unrighteousness (Rom. 1:18–23). Instead of listening to the word of truth, they incline their ears to the siren songs of the devil, the father of lies, who is a liar from the beginning (John 8:44).

The Organization of Ideas

Philosophy, as the love of wisdom, also implies that there are specific truths held in possession. To be wise is to have in one's grasp certain information or propositions that can be articulated either orally or on paper. To have a philosophy of education is to have and hold to a variety of ideas or propositions about the sundry aspects of the pedagogic process. A philosopher, whether of the amateur or the professional variety, must have some ideas about

- the means to measure academic success,
- the role of the teacher,
- the nature and function of the curriculum,
- the nature of the learning process,
- the nature of the persons to be educated,
- measuring or evaluating whether true education has occurred.

The possibilities are numerous, even though the typical amateur may be hard-pressed to articulate all the ideas latent in his subliminal experience.

It should be apparent that the ideas about education cannot be thrown into a mixing bowl and flung together in some random, haphazard fashion. Some ideas have consequence for others. Some ideas are predicated on a set of assumptions that need to be articulated as part of the validation process. Some ideas will even determine the nature of subsequent choices. To pretend that one can make wise judgments about measuring effectiveness without first having defined the objectives being pursued is folly. One must know what is being attempted before one can determine whether the effort has been successful. To determine whether or not one has learned must be preceded by an understanding of the nature of learning, for that is implicit in the evaluation.

One of the most popular and highly respected books published in the United States was an old volume by Ralph W. Tyler called *Basic Principles of Curriculum and Instruction.*[2] This book, comprising only 128 pages, went through no fewer than thirty printings and propelled its author to the status of being one of the most influential thinkers in American education. It still is a prime mover in the world of teacher training. Tyler began the book by asking four simple questions:

1. What educational purposes should the school seek to attain?
2. What educational experiences can be provided that are likely to attain these purposes?
3. How can these educational experiences be effectively organized?
4. How can we determine whether these purposes are being attained?[3]

As an educational philosopher, I must admit that I never heard of this classic until almost two decades after I had organized and published *Education in the Truth.*[4] To the best of my knowledge, I was not influenced by Tyler's ideas or philosophical scheme. At the same time there is a great deal of common sense in what Tyler has written. Many ideas have consequences for others, and it makes a significant difference in which order we ask questions. Tyler put some foundational questions in the right sequence. For that he is to be commended.

But Tyler is also to be critiqued. To accept his philosophy as being true and worthy of emulation would be to make a critical mistake. Tyler has asked some questions that the Christian must also ask. But he has failed to address other matters that the non-Christian seems unwilling to ask. In the words of Cornelius Van Til,[5] this popular humanist has failed to own up to a number of crucial presuppositions or assumptions, without the articulation of which his scheme is hollow and vacuous. Tyler jumps into the middle of the pedagogic process without ever posing questions about the existing nature of the educand who is supposed to undergo the behavioral changes that he recommends. If there is an ideal or desired state of affairs that the educator hopes to attain, there must also be an existing state of affairs that is judged to be unsatisfactory. There is not only an "ought" condition, but also there must be an "is" condition. What is the nature of the child that necessitates some kind of change? What are the attributes of human beings that are so undesirable as to necessitate an expensive, decade-long process whose primary purpose is to produce measurable changes? To borrow the words of David,

> What is man that You are mindful of him
> And the son of man that You visit him? (Ps. 8:4)

Tyler doesn't ask the question, and neither do his countless disciples, because they have an assumed set of answers that they would prefer not to expose to public scrutiny. To ask the question requires that answers be offered and evaluated. Sometimes it is easier not to ask the question.

A second set of questions that Tyler fails to address is that of responsibility. He never asks who is to be responsible for conducting and guiding the educational process, who is to determine which objectives are valid and important. Tyler does not ask the question because he uncritically assumes that the public school, as an agent of the state, has that responsibility. He is an ardent apologist for public schools in the tradition of John Dewey and Horace Mann. Again, to ask the question would be to suggest that there might be multiple answers, most of which would contradict his presupposed position. Better to carry the assumption forward under wraps than to risk debilitating debate and possible loss of power.

A third, and probably the most significant of all, question that

Tyler chooses not to acknowledge is the one that asks, By whose authority do you make those decisions? The Jews of Jesus' day often peppered Him with that type of question. In response to Jesus' teaching in the temple, "the chief priests, the scribes, and the elders came to Him. And they said to Him, 'By what authority are You doing these things? And who gave You this authority to do these things?'" (Mark 11:27–28; cf. Matt. 21:23–27; John 5:26–28; Luke 20:1–8).

The Jews of Jesus' day were reprimanded not for asking the question but for refusing to accept the answer that was proffered. Jesus repeatedly told them that He had been sent by the Father and that He had been commissioned by the Holy Spirit, but they refused to believe Him. They would not accept Him as an authority because they would not believe that He was the Son of God, part of the Trinity. The question therefore is legitimate and must be asked by everyone seriously concerned with educational practice. Those of us who are Christians have to ask it not only of ourselves but also of each other. In the current milieu it is popular for some Christian pedagogues to condemn all approaches to the teaching of reading skills except that of the phonics method. Some highly respected and popular spokespersons for home schooling and for Christian schools contend vigorously that the reason for academic demise has been the abandonment of the phonics method. They also contend, mistakenly, that the best cure for academic deficiency is a return to that phonics method.

These friends of the faith are entitled to their opinions, but they also must be lovingly questioned, "By what authority do you make that judgment?" That is not an inappropriate question, even though it could be asked in inappropriate tones. The world is full of conflicting and contradictory opinions. Which ones do we accept as truthful, and on what basis do we come to that conclusion? Anyone who has studied the history of education ought to know that there are strongly held differences of opinion about almost all matters affecting education. To not raise the question of authority is to be irresponsible.

But Christians must not only ask the question of themselves and fellow Christians. They must also ask it of the powerful humanistic system that controls the public schools of the land. The question must be asked of every historian, every psychologist, every philosopher, every administrator, and every classroom teacher: Are we operating our schools in the fashion that we are because the state superintendent of schools has said that we should? Are we choosing our objectives because they have been promulgated by Dewey? Are we leaving Christ out of the classroom because Mann cleverly disguised his Unitarian theology as a humanitarian desire for absence of conflict? Are we treating students as empty buckets waiting to be filled with our endless supply of knowledge because Jean Jacques Rousseau saw a child as a tabula rasa? Are we choosing to ignore questions about the nature of the educand and the locus of authority because Tyler taught us to ignore them?

A System of Addressing Issues

In the late 1960s, when my college president commissioned me to draft a philosophy of education for our Christian schools, God revealed to me a system for arranging questions that has met the test of time. Since the publication of *Education in the Truth,* no one has ever seriously questioned the basic philosophic structure around which that book was built. To this date, I have been convinced that those ideas are derived from God's Word and fully compatible with it. The precise choice of terms is open to various options, but the sequence in which those questions need to be asked is firm. When they are combined with each other, we will have a philosophy of education that should prove to be testable, valid, functional, and in complete harmony with the very Authority on which it is based.

The questions can be asked in either a backward or a forward fashion. We can begin with evaluative queries about the quality of our educational system and then work backward through a series of assumptions to the source. Or we can begin with questions about the foundation for our schools and then work forward to a system for measuring the effectiveness of the program. For the sake of clarity, both approaches will be utilized here.

The Backward Approach

1. Is that a good school? Is that teacher accomplishing what he or she ought? Are the students learning what they ought? Is the school doing its job?

Evaluation:
Was the task performed properly and effectively?

2. Who is responsible for teaching that? Was that a task properly assigned to the school? Can we hold the school responsible if the job was given to the parents? What role did the church and the state have to play?

Responsibility:
Who is responsible?

3. By what means, or methods, was the task attempted? Were those responsible using the most efficient tools and methods for attempting the task?

Methodology:
Were the most efficient tools and materials employed?

4. What specific goals or objectives were being attempted? Were those the most important, valuable goals that could have been chosen? Who chose them? How were they chosen?

Objectives, goals, or ends:
What should be learned?

5. What is the existing nature of the learner that makes these goals necessary? Why should the child be coerced to try to attain those objectives? What are the primary characteristics of the student that make these goals important?

The nature of the students:
What are the children like?

6. On what authority are all of the preceding questions answered? Who has so much insight that we can trust him with these very significant questions? Where can we go, without embarrassment, to find the answers?

By what authority:
Who has all the answers?

The Foundational Approach

Another way to address the matter of educational philosophy is to use the analogy of building a house. One has to start somewhere and to perform the variety of tasks necessary toward completion in some sort of systematic way. It would be the height of folly to begin the construction process by putting in doors or windows or by first installing the appliances. It would be even more ridiculous if one suggested that the first step in construction would be the laying of shingles. Obviously the first step in any construction project is the laying of some sort of foundation. That foundation will determine the shape and size of the home. It will determine whether the house will sustain the storms that will almost certainly come its way. The foundation will not be readily seen once the superstructure has been built upon it, but it will always be there.

In our construction of an educational philosophy, the first and most basic action will be the establishment of a foundation. It will be the beginning point, or basis, upon which all subsequent action will build. In time, the foundation may be hidden from view and not be easily recognized or identified. But it will continue, and it will serve the function of determining all future educational activity. It can be called the starting point, the foundation, the basis, or the ultimate authority. I prefer the last term, for all those engaged in pedagogic analysis appeal to some author or authority beyond themselves.

From this ultimate authority we can derive answers to that most significant question about the nature of man. Paraphrasing David's concern, we need to ask, "What is the nature of the person to be educated? What are the primary qualities or characteristics that I need to know in order to teach him most efficiently? Is the child born with original sin, as the Bible teaches? Is the child born without any sin, merely a blank slate, or a tabula rasa, as John Locke, Rousseau, and their countless followers insist? Is the person merely a product of his environment, shaped and formed whichever way the cultural winds of his day and place determine? Is the child pure as driven snow until such time as his culture corrupts him?" Such questions are crucial to the educational process, for the answers to such will largely determine what goals will be chosen and how the child will respond to them.

The third set of questions that needs to be asked concerns the choice of learning goals. A goal, in life as well as in sports, is something toward which one strives. Sundry names have been used in conjunction with this pursuit, and they should not confuse the student. Whether we call these goals, objectives, aims, ends, purposes, or ends in view is of no particular consequence. The concept is clear: Any one of these synonyms is something toward which we strive but which we do not necessarily attain. Basketball teams try to put the ball through the basket every time, but they seldom are more than 50 percent successful. There are obvious reasons for such lack of success, because there are opponents to conquer and resistance to overcome.

The formulation of goals or ends is of the greatest significance, for there are scores of competing systems begging for adoption. There are numerous forces wanting to impose their goals on the process in order to gain control of those who wield future power. The allies of the devil are ever busy in a lifelong battle for the souls and minds of men. This world is not a friend to God but is in open rebellion against Him. Furthermore, the articulation of goals implies that there is some ideal or desired state for the educand, in contrast to the present, existing condition in which we find the child. The *ought* is to be preferred to the *is*. His *becoming* is of more consequence than is his *being*.

The fourth set of concerns is that of assigning responsibility for the accomplishment of these goals. In the construction industry, the general contractor will seek out and employ subcontractors to take responsibility for various facets of the building process. He will hire an architect to draw up blueprints from which the contractors can submit bids. He will then select framers, electricians, cement layers, plumbers, roofers, and finish carpenters to help him complete the project. Each will be given specific responsibility for specific tasks.

Each will then become accountable to the general contractor for the performance of those duties.

The same is true in the realm of education. If "children are a heritage from the LORD" (Ps. 127:3), then the Lord becomes the master Builder, the rock from which His living stones are hewn (1 Peter 2:4–5; 1 Kings 6:7). He is the one who assigns the various tasks to be performed. To the parents goes the primary responsibility for education, because God has seen fit to have children born into homes, within the bounds of marriage, and commands those children to honor their fathers and mothers as the primary authority under which they are to learn. This does not exclude the church or the state from exercising some authority, for they too are given specific areas of responsibility.

The fifth set of concerns is that involving methodological questions. If one of our primary goals for the child is to teach him to love, honor, and obey those in authority over him, how can that be accomplished? If we don't know how to reach that objective or if we do not recognize it as an important end to be reached, there is high probability that the student will not arrive there. Obviously the choice of goals will go far to determine the methods to be employed. If the Christian teacher recognizes that discernment between truth and falsehood is a primary goal for the student, it would not be in anyone's best interest if the teacher promoted unsupervised and unevaluated reading or watching of videos. To allow teenagers uninterrupted access to the television or the Internet, with nary an analysis or a rebuke for what is being watched, would almost certainly not promote discernment.

In the realms of reading, math, writing, and music skills, there are societies and journals devoted to the matters of methodology. Some teachers never get beyond such concerns, and some novice education students think that such is the only legitimate concern for their training programs. Methodology does make a difference and is a legitimate concern, but it should not be addressed until all of the preceding issues have been put into proper focus. Only as a teacher sees clearly the primary tasks that God has assigned to His children can we begin to ask questions about the most efficient and effective ways to reach those goals.

The sixth and final set of questions is that which asks whether we have reached our goals. Did the school accomplish what it was assigned? Did it follow the blueprint that the Architect and Builder had laid out? Will God, whose children have been entrusted to their care, be pleased? Will He say, "Well done, good and faithful servant" (Matt. 25:21)? Will He bless their efforts and assign them to more duties? Will He employ them again?

We can illustrate this by the following philosophical ladder. A comparison of this formulation with that of the backward approach will show that the concepts and the sequence are the same, with only an alteration in the wording and in the analogies used.

Evaluation:
How good is the school?

Methodology:
How can we most effectively reach those goals?

Responsible agency:
Who is responsible for education?

Goals, objectives, or aims:
What should the child become?

The nature of the student:
What is the child like?

Ultimate authority, basis, or foundation

The issue of quality control and quality assessment is not disconnected from all the questions that have gone before. Ultimately the determination of whether a school is good or bad, whether it is to be commended or whether it is to be condemned, will be decided by the One who has authority over that school. The One who has laid down the terms of the contract and who has either drawn or commissioned the blueprint will have the right to decide whether any school deserves the label of good, bad, awful, or excellent.

By What Authority?

> Now when He came into the temple, the chief priests and the elders of the people confronted Him as He was teaching, and said, "By what authority are You doing these things? And who gave You this authority?"
>
> But Jesus answered and said to them, "I also will ask you one thing, which if you tell Me, I likewise will tell you by what authority I do these things: The baptism of John—where was it from? From heaven or from men?"
>
> And they reasoned among themselves, saying, "If we say, 'From heaven,' He will say to us, 'Why then did you not believe him?' But if we say, 'From men,' we fear the multitude, for all count John as a prophet." So they answered Jesus and said, "We do not know."
>
> And He said to them, "Neither will I tell you by what authority I do these things." (Matt. 21:23–27)

This challenge from the Jewish leaders to the Messiah is one of great significance. The question itself is a responsible one, for anyone making the claim to be the promised Savior of the world could expect to be confronted with questions about the foundation for such a claim. Jesus Christ does not fault the chief priests and elders of the church for asking a legitimate question. Nowhere does He reply or even imply that it is foolish. On the contrary, He turns the question around and directs it back to them. In His wisdom, Jesus suggests that the question is basic and forces them to address it seriously. His debate is not with the question they asked but with their persistent rejection of the answer He had given them.

Jesus is in His final days before offering Himself as the Lamb to be slain. He knows the intense hatred of the religious leaders; He knows that they are going to charge Him with blasphemy because He has dared to claim that He is the Son of God. The Master has repeatedly made the claim that He is speaking the Father's words and that He is doing what He does because it is the Father's will. That assertion was categorically rejected by the Jewish leaders, with few exceptions. When they confronted Him again in the temple, they were hoping that He would give the answer that they could use to convict Him in their church courts. But Jesus was too smart for them. His time was not quite yet.

The Pedagogical Inquiry

Whenever we engage in significant analysis and assessment of educational practice, we need to ask the same question of those who are trying to implement their program or defend a system under attack. If, for example, we find some group, either in our community or on a larger scale, advocating character education, we need to ask, "By what authority do you make those claims?" To put it another way, we should inquire as to the foundation or the basis for their assertions.

I believe that schools ought to be concerned with the character development of their students, but I need to know much more before I want to jump on that proverbial bandwagon. What is meant by character education? Whose version of character education will be implemented? Will such a program negate the value of developing marketable skills? Will it diminish the importance of transmitting the Judeo-Christian cultural heritage? Will it substitute for a specifically Christocentric focus and put the spotlight on behavior modification with a middle-class twist?

Those who come armed with new educational programs, especially during times of crisis, need to be viewed with caution, lest we absorb some new agenda that is no better than the one it is supposed to replace. Character education, even as advanced by William Bennett, stops short of addressing a child's greatest need. Those who want to develop virtues will need to ask not only, "What virtues?" but also "By what authority and power, and for what motive?" What is often lacking in character education is the biblical emphasis on the centrality of Jesus Christ. Although Bennett's writings are welcome calls to recover morality, is that all Christians need to bring up their children in the fear and nurture of the Lord?

Dewey articulated his foundational beliefs about the nature of education in a paper called "My Pedagogic Creed." In the opening lines of that famous treatise he argued,

> All education proceeds by the participation of the individual in the social consciousness of the race. This process begins unconsciously almost at birth, and is continually shaping the individual's powers, saturating his consciousness, forming his habits, training his ideas, and arousing his feelings and emotions. . . . The only true education comes through the stimulation of the child's powers by the demands of the social situations in which he finds himself. . . . The child's own instincts and powers furnish the material and give the starting point for all education.[6]

For Dewey there was only one foundation upon which true education could be built: the experiences of the individual. Not willing to concede the starting point to the society or the culture into which the individual is born, Dewey insisted that man is self-starting, self-governing, and self-directed. The foundation for education is autonomous man, who carves his own interpretations out of the experiences he encounters, who builds his own values, and who creates his own choices. For this man who had forsaken the God of his mother and who had rejected the teachings of Christianity, each child is his own master, the guardian of his own soul.

But no man is an island. No man is so great that he can stand alone. Even a person so influential as Dewey had to admit that his ideas were not original but were borrowed heavily from those who had preceded him. Dewey could argue that the highest purpose of education was to produce "democratic citizens" who could adapt to their ever-changing culture. He could argue that man is, in his essential nature, nothing more than a social resultant, a product of his environment, but Dewey could not argue that on his own authority. He again was borrowing from prior authors. When pressed, he had to admit that those thoughts were not original but were transcribed from such intellectual sources as Rousseau and Karl Marx and Charles Darwin. They in turn had lifted their ideas from such earlier sources as Hegel, Spinoza, and Aristotle. He also had to admit that his primary ideas were the categorical rejection of all things Platonic or Pauline. What Dewey was forced to admit is a truth that all of us must acknowledge. We are dependent for our ideas and our theories on some source outside ourselves. When pressed, we go to authorities that we respect for support and clarification. We know, albeit subconsciously, that we cannot stand for long by ourselves, on our own authority. We need a higher, more powerful source from which to draw strength and courage.

For the Christian, that authority is none other than God Himself. We recognize Him as the all-powerful One, the omniscient One, the Creator, the Provider, the sovereign King of the universe, the One who "is before all things, and in Him all things consist" (Col. 1:17). We go to Him, the Author of the Bible, for all the important questions of life, knowing that His Word is "so clearly propounded, and opened in some place of Scripture or other, that not only the learned, but the unlearned, in a due use of the ordinary means, may attain unto a sufficient understanding of them" (Westminster Confession of Faith, 1.7). Beyond the pages of Scripture we cannot find a higher authority, a more reliable, definitive source, for there is none greater, more knowledgeable, more informed than God Himself. Adhering to the Reformed doctrine of *sola Scriptura*, we believe that "the infallible rule of interpretation of Scripture is the Scripture itself; and therefore, when there is a question about the true and full sense of any Scripture (which is not manifold, but one), it must be searched and known by other places that speak more clearly" (Westminster Confession, 1.9). In the language of another, older Reformed tradition, "We believe that those scriptures fully contain the will of God, and that whatsoever man ought to believe unto salvation is sufficiently taught therein" (Belgic Confession of Faith, art. 7).

Does that mean that every question an educator faces ought to be researched in the pages of the Bible? Is God to be consulted on every issue that may trouble a teacher or an administrator? The obvious answer is no, for no map needs to be so detailed as to mark every possible road, trail, or path. Just as a road map includes only those main roads or streets that one needs to get from point A to point B, so the Bible does not trivialize life by telling us whether high schools should be one story or two stories in height or whether the purchasing agent should order yellow buses or orange ones. If a state law were involved, however, mandating only the purchase of orange buses, then God's Word will speak to the issue, for He tells us, "Let every soul be subject to the governing authorities. For there is no authority except from God, and the authorities that exist are appointed by God" (Rom. 13:1).

Whenever we address any questions of importance, we all, Christian and non-Christian alike, inevitably turn to some higher authority in whom we have confidence. The non-Christian moralist may turn to Plato, to Shakespeare, to George Washington, or to William Bennett, but always appealing to someone beyond himself. The one who has come to worship the gospel of democracy will turn to the words of Thomas Jefferson, Dewey, or William Jefferson Clinton. The Unitarian Universalist will turn to the writings of Thomas Paine, Mann, or Bertrand Russell, while a Calvinist will employ the concepts of John Calvin, John Knox, Abraham Kuyper, or Cornelius Van Til.

Vast numbers of people make their appeal to science, without ever knowing what or whom that word represents. Science has a powerful appeal and has been ascribed almost unquestioned authority, so that countless debates are stultified by unexamined appeals to this god of the twentieth century.[7] In earlier eras, the appeal often was to reason, again without a clarification of what was meant or how answers could be validated. People then as now put their faith—a blind faith—in reason or in science, hoping thereby to find authority for their stance.[8]

——— 3 How Do We Find Answers?

Then Jesus said to those Jews who believed Him, "If you abide in My word, you are My disciples indeed. And you shall know the truth, and the truth shall set you free." (John 8:31–32)

For a long time the majority of us believed that if something was once found to be true, it was always true. Ideas that were considered true by our grandparents were also considered true by our parents, so we accepted them as true also. We consequently passed them on to our children and hoped that they would do the same. What was true for Abraham was true for David, and what was true for David was true for Paul. What was true for Paul was good enough for Father and therefore good enough for me.

All Truth Is Absolute

To think that way is to believe that truth is absolute. In a culture dominated by the Judeo-Christian tradition and governed intellectually by the dictates of Platonic philosophy, absolutism was quietly assumed. What was true yesterday is true today and will be tomorrow. What is false today will be false tomorrow.

That way of looking at truth is coming under increasing attack, not only in our universities but also in our seminaries and in our pulpits. Countless ministers are claiming that the Bible is culturally conditioned. What was acceptable for Paul was okay for him but cannot be considered acceptable today. The role of women in church office is but one example of such a shift in paradigm. Whereas Paul made it plain that women should be silent in the church and that only mature males might qualify for ecclesiastical office, the vast majority of evangelical churches in the Western world find such teaching to be time warped and out of harmony with current thought. Even concerning homosexuality, where both the Old and New Testaments speak with unmistakable clarity, many mainline Protestant churches find it not only necessary but even essential to embrace practicing homosexuals. To inquire of such churches whether truth is absolute would be to draw a laugh of derision.

To make the claim that all truth is absolute is to assert that what is true on any given day will always be true, no matter what the conditions or the context. Without being fully prepared to defend that truth, we hung on to it, and then came the onslaughts of empirical science. It is the nature of scientific effort, we are told, to disprove the propositions of yesterday and to advance the cause of knowledge one step at a time. The mark of true science[1] is that it is tentative and not absolute. As men discovered more and more about the universe in which they lived, they were forced to conclude that the old truths were no longer true. Especially under the influence of the empiricists John Locke and David Hume (and later, the Logical Positivists) and the pragmatists William James and John Dewey, the notion of absolute truth was gradually eroded. For the empiricists, truth depends on perceptions, and perceptions change with time. For the pragmatists, whatever works, whatever produces desirable observable consequences, is true and worthy of acceptance. Gone are the overarching absolutes that once guided us. Everything, the relativists say, is relative. Nothing is absolute.

Such an assertion is a clever lie, for the people who shout most loudly that "there are no absolutes" treat that very claim as an unchanging, absolute truth. For the relativists to insist absolutely that there are no absolutes is for them to put forth an absolute, thus contradicting their own claim.

Another way to test the veracity of relativists is to search their writings for other assertions that are always, in all contexts, purported to be true. Dewey, the leading American philosopher of the twentieth century, was notorious for advancing absolutes while claiming to be doing the opposite. He saw science as universally good, the best road to truth. Evolution too was, for him, indisputably the best, most valid explanation of the universe. Because it is the antithesis of creation, he was sure of the universal truth of evolution and the universal falsehood of creation, thus giving us two more absolutes. Standing above all other absolutes is the absolute of democracy. With passionate hatred for kings and kingdoms, Dewey insisted that the greatest virtue toward which all persons must strive is that of democracy. For him, in life as in chess, the primary goal was to eliminate the king.

In the twentieth century, the absolute of democracy ruled governmental policy and led to numerous military engagements. World War I, we all said, was fought to make the world safe for democracy. In more recent decades, military incursions by the United States and its democratic allies into Haiti, Somalia, Iraq, Serbia, Northern Ireland, Kosovo, and Israel have all been justified in the name of preserving or extending the reach of democracy. Implicit in those actions is the proposition that man is and must remain autonomous, that all men deserve to be free and self-governing. No one has exemplified this more passionately than William Jefferson Clinton. For him, as for most Americans, democracy trumps both truth and justice.

On a parallel note, we have encountered a new absolute in the last decade of the second millennium. In an era when choice, privacy, and sexual preference have become the defining ideals of our culture, toleration has emerged as the latest absolute. To be most tolerant is to be most virtuous. Josh McDowell has expressed it well. He writes,

> My son Sean was a high school senior when I asked, "Son, in 12 years of public school, were you ever taught that anything is absolutely true?"
>
> "Sure," he said.
>
> Surprised, I asked him what absolute truth he had learned.
>
> He shrugged, "Tolerance."
>
> I have since discovered that Sean's experience is common. Tolerance has become the cardinal virtue, the sole absolute of our society, and our children hear it preached every

day in school and from government and the media. Yet few of us understand what society really means by tolerance, nor do we realize that it is the central doctrine of an entire cultural movement. As a result, few of us recognize the threat it poses to us, our children, our churches and our very faith.[2]

On a Less Grand Scale

To claim that some grand, philosophical truths are absolute is fairly easy to do. But to claim that all truth is absolute is to fly in the face of the most powerful philosophies of our secular society. Those who dominate our universities, colleges, and public schools are not even willing to concede that truth is real. For those awash in Hegelian dialectics, in Darwinian evolution, or in postmodern subjectivism, nothing is fixed and firm. Nothing is known with certainty or permanence. To claim that all truth is absolute is to invite ridicule and revenge.

To buttress our claim, therefore, we must move on from the sublime to the ridiculous. We must move out of the realm of the divine into the mundane affairs of daily life, from the "eternal verities" so roundly ridiculed by Dewey to those little truths that make up our common existence. Take for example a daily weather report. We can turn on our radio or our television, or we can pick up the daily paper, and discover that it was 94 degrees in Chicago at 3:00 P.M. on July 30, 1999. Based on experiences in that city over the past twenty years, that fact is not hard to believe. Without so much as a critical glance, we accept the report as true.

Fair enough, relativists might argue, but that little truth is good only for a very short time. Within an hour, the temperature reading will probably be down to 91 degrees, and then it will plunge into the sixties or seventies by midnight. Our supposed eternal verity was only temporal.

In one limited sense, we would not want to argue, for temperatures are subject to fluctuation. For that we can be eternally grateful. But in another very real sense, that original statement is and will be forever true.

On July 30, 1999, at the official reading station at O'Hare Airport, the temperature did register 94 degrees. Certain assumed conditions are included in that calculation: (1) the use of a Fahrenheit gauge and not Celsius, (2) central daylight savings time and not standard time, (3) that the temperature could have been different at other reporting stations within the city. Given all of that, it is truthful to say that on that date, at that hour, at that official reporting location, the temperature did reach the 94-degree mark. That statement, with those assumed qualifiers, will be true tomorrow, next year, next decade, and next century, should the Lord tarry that long. The statement, no matter how trivial, is and always will be true. It, like the grandest, most profound wisdom of Scripture, is absolutely true. Its truth will not change.

All Truth Is Relative

The following simple quiz will help us to see that, in another sense, all truth is relative. Please take a moment and answer these questions as either true or false.

_____ 1. The coldest month of the year is usually January.
_____ 2. South winds are almost always warm winds.
_____ 3. Moss grows on the north side of trees.
_____ 4. Christmas is celebrated in the middle of the winter.
_____ 5. Temperatures are colder the farther north you go.
_____ 6. The longest day of the year occurs on June 21.

If you answered true to these questions, you probably live in the northern hemisphere and have never experienced living in the southern hemisphere. If you answered false to all of the questions, you may be a native of Australia, South Africa, or Argentina. Whether or not the above statements are true is determined by one's relationship to the equator. If you live south of the equator, as we did for a while, you begin to realize that what you assumed to be true in the northern hemisphere is the opposite in the southern. At first that is a disconcerting experience, but you gradually come to understand that all such matters as climate, direction, and seasons are radically affected by one's relationship to the equator.

Our grab bag of relative truths is not limited to matters affected by their location in one hemisphere or the other. Let us try a few more quiz items and see how we fare on these.

_____ 7. Green Lake in Wisconsin is a very large lake.

_____ 8. If you travel north in a straight line, you will always be traveling north.

_____ 9. Ninety years is an unusually long lifespan.

_____10. On June 21, the sun usually rises at approximately 5:28 A.M. and sets at approximately 9:43 P.M.

A simple true or false answer to any of the preceding questions is certain to raise a vigorous dissent with most astute persons. It is true that Green Lake in Wisconsin is a very large lake when compared with Indian Lake at Howard City, Michigan, but it is patently false when compared with Lake Superior or any other of the Great Lakes. Size is obviously relative to that which is larger or smaller.

The eighth question is also problematic. If you begin at almost any point on the earth's surface, you can travel in a northerly direction. But if you keep traveling north, you will eventually reach the North Pole. From that point, there is only one direction you can go, and that is south. If you are standing on the North Pole, you cannot go north, east, or west, but only south. All matters of direction, whether north or south or east or west, are determined in relationship to some point of reference.

A ninety-year lifespan, in twentieth-century terms, is a long time, assuming that one is talking about human beings. If the reference, however, is to trees, or to dogs, or to mosquitoes, the span of life takes on a whole new meaning. But even among humans, ninety years is nothing more than childhood if the reference point is the life of Methuselah, who lived to the ripe old age of 969 years (Gen. 5:27).

Question 10, like the first six questions, assumes that the respondent is living in the northern hemisphere. The statement also assumes that we are operating on daylight savings time rather than on Greenwich standard time. It furthermore assumes that we are living and thinking somewhere near the forty-third latitude north, in the vicinity of such major cities as Chicago, Detroit, and New York. If you travel north to the Arctic Circle on that same date, the time of sunrise and sunset will change dramatically, even to the extent of there being no sunset or sunrise. If you travel to the south, near to the equator, the sun will rise much later than 5:28 A.M. and will set much earlier than 9:30 P.M. All matters of climate and weather, like those of direction and distance, are affected by location and reference point.

One of Western culture's recognized geniuses is Albert Einstein, a German-born physicist who lived from 1879 to 1955. He is most noted for his theory of relativity, which most writers studiously avoid discussing and most people do not understand. Endowed by his Creator with an extraordinary insight into the cohesive nature of the physical universe, Einstein spent much of his early adult life critiquing the theories of Isaac Newton (1642–1727), a noted Christian physicist. Focusing his primary attention on the nature and relationship of physical properties, Einstein was convinced that the principles of Newtonian physics were in error.

Pared down to its most essential format, Einstein's proposition is that nothing can be understood in isolation. Everything exists in some kind of context, which necessitates seeing things in relationship to something else in order to understand them. Simply put, everything is relative. To perceive anything accurately (i.e., truthfully), we must see it in reference to something else. Nothing stands alone. Nothing can be understood alone.

In 1940, in response to the outbreak of World War II in Europe, many of the intellectual leaders of the West gathered in New York City for a conference on "Science, Philosophy and Religion." Among them was Einstein, who argued that "the conflict between science and religion could not be resolved, and hence true unity cannot be achieved unless religious people give up the idea of a personal God."[3] His conclusions were probably shared by many of the conferees, none of whom were noted as Calvinist stalwarts, for modernistic thought was already deeply entrenched in American culture.

Such a categorical rejection of a personal God, however, gave Einstein a reputation and an image that made him persona non grata with Bible-believing Christians. To reject the sovereign Creator of the universe, the One who alone is transcendent to all that He has made, is to discard the only referent qualified to give meaning to everything in the world. Instead of seeing the triune God as the center of the universe, the One in whom all things consist and have their being, Einstein remained true to his democratic ideology.

For many Christians, the response was quick, simple, and dirty. All of those associated with the conference were categorically wrong. Einstein, Dewey, and all of their humanistic secularist cohorts had again attempted to put man in God's place. Democracy, as the highest hope of sinful man, is the presumptive displacement of a sovereign God by an arrogant, autonomous human race. Their answer must be loudly rejected.

It was not difficult for Dewey, Boyd Bode, William Heard Kilpatrick, and a host of other progressive educators to accept Einstein's view. Suppressing the truth in unrighteousness, all of those committed to secular humanism were ready and anxious to preach the gospel of democracy and to fight a second world war to make the world safe for democracy. Waging ideological war against "all truth is absolute," they insisted instead that "all truth is relative."

Einstein and his ilk were fundamentally in error. In clear, unmistakable terms, the choice was between two simplistic yet potent pronouncements: "All truth is absolute" or "All truth is relative." To be a Christian was to reject everything that Dewey, Einstein, and every other progressive ever uttered. To be a Christian was to choose for absolutism and against relativism.

But the options are not that simple. To choose against relativism is to miss the meaning of Paul's letter to the Colossian Christians, where he writes,

> He [Christ] is the image of the invisible God, the firstborn over all creation. For by Him all things were created that are in heaven and that are on earth, visible and invisible, whether thrones or dominions or principalities or powers. All things were created through Him and for Him. And He is before all things, and in Him all things consist. (Col. 1:15–17)

Paul is pointedly telling them and us that God's Son, Jesus Christ, is the center, the source, and the reference point for everything that exists or that can be conceived. God-centered education, in contrast to child-centered, man-centered, or subject-centered education, is the only type that can be judged true, for it is true to God.

What the humanists have done is to put themselves at the center of existence, to claim for themselves the authority, the power, and the purposes that rightfully belong to God. The secular humanist not only eliminates God from the equation but also puts himself in God's place. He says that all truth is relative, but when questioned as to what or to whom it is relative, he insists that it is relative to himself. The humanist is wrong not because he insists that all truth must be seen in relationship to a reference point but because he insists on making himself the reference point. In philosophic terms, that is subjectivism, pure, simple, and false.

Christians must recognize that all those who reject Jesus Christ are children of the devil, as Jesus so pointedly told the Jewish leaders (John 8:44). To be a son or daughter of Satan is to be a liar, one who distorts and perverts the truth constantly. To lie is not to replace the truth with its opposite, nor is it to deny its existence. To lie is to twist the truth, to distort it in such a way that it will not acknowledge the divinity of Jesus Christ, the existence of God, and the centrality of His claims to sovereignty. To lie is to put man or the devil or someone else in God's place and to make a new point of reference. To lie is to twist the truth for human, personal advantage.

Subjectivism is a bald-faced lie that must be renounced. Humanism is a variation of subjectivism, which is at war with biblical theology. Democracy, as the theology of humanists and as an approach to life, is a claim that man is autonomous and is responsible and accountable to no one except to himself. Democracy, as a rejection of kingships everywhere, is antithetical to Christianity. Christ preached the message of the kingdom constantly. Those committed to democracy want to eliminate the king, as though they were playing chess. As the source of all truth, the King tells us to watch out for the perversions of all those who would reject Him.

For Christians to be very wary of relativity theories is commendable. But to juxtapose those relativity theories as the opposite of absolutist theories is to commit a serious mistake. The truth is not either absolute or relative.

The truth, when understood as God's revelation of His wisdom, is both absolute and relative. Such a conclusion is not a capitulation to Einstein's and Dewey's views but a godly correction of them. Truth is both eternal and cohesive; it is fixed and reliable while never existing in isolation. To recognize that truth is both absolute and relative is to begin to see the world in a unified, holistic fashion, shaped and given meaning by its Creator God. To make such a claim is to begin to comprehend the importance of God-centered education.

Who Are Scientists?

We were sitting around the lunchroom table, five of us in all. We had been ruminating about a discussion held two days earlier in our monthly faculty forum. The topic had been the creation-evolution debate, hardly a dead issue on most campuses. In response to some impassioned remarks about scientists, I asked a colleague who had been most vociferous, "How many scientists are at this table?"

He looked rather pensive for a few seconds and then said, "One."

"Who is it?" I asked, with a twinkle in my eye.

His reply surprised me only a little. I knew he didn't think of me as a scientist, for I specialized in training future teachers. I knew that he wasn't thinking of himself, for he prided himself on being an artist. And I did not expect him to label the two psychology professors, even though they were openly hoping that he would point to them and had forgotten how to count.

He finally pointed at a professor of obstetrical nursing, who was more than a little surprised. "Why me?" she asked.

"You are a scientist because you are at least partially involved in the field of medicine."

By now all five minds were in high gear. Why did she deserve that distinction? Why isn't psychology a science? Why isn't education a science? Why don't you deserve to be called a scientist if you deliberately and frequently employ the scientific method?

The problem is that no one bothers to define science. We keep using a term that no one, including those who proudly call themselves scientists, begins or even tries to understand. The situation is almost as ridiculous as having a devious teacher go to a preschool and chant repeatedly to three-year-olds, "You are all philanthropists" until they've memorized the word and could repeat it in every conceivable encounter. We would look askance and wonder who had planted this meaningless term in their heads.

When we use the word *science* without the faintest notion of its meaning, we are no different from those three year olds. Yet the words *science* and *scientific* have become tremendously significant words in our culture. The intellectual climate is such that the mere designation "scientist" almost magically entitles one to high praise for possession of marvelous new discoveries. To be unscientific, by contrast, is to be uninformed at best or stupid and senseless at worst. To charge a person with being unscientific is to heap coals of condemnation on his head.

For many people, *science* always must be capitalized. Science, if not possessing divine qualities, is a powerful, personal force capable of curing cancer, discovering new chemical elements, dating fossils, and sending space shuttles into orbit. Science can accomplish almost anything. For such people, science is to be worshiped, not defined.

For the Christian, however, such an attitude is unacceptable. The holy and jealous God of the Scriptures would never brook such presumptuous deification or even the lesser evil of personification. God did not create science in His image or make it a little lower than the angels. No, science falls into some other category. For Christians, at least, science must be defined, not worshiped.

A perusal of any standard dictionary will indicate that the root meaning of *science* is "knowledge." In Latin we find the words *scientia*, *sciens*, and *scire*, which were translated respectively as "knowledge," "knowing," and "to know." This classical meaning has been transmitted down through the ages into Western culture and was utilized by the English, French, and Germans with little variation in meaning until the middle of the nineteenth century.

Knowledge, or science, was something to be acquired or something that one could hold in possession, but it never took on personal or divine qualities. Everyone would have looked askance, for example, if anyone had labeled a person who had acquired some knowledge as being a knowledgist. Yet that is essentially what Reverend William Whewell, a Cambridge philosopher of science, attempted in

1834. He coined the word *scientist* but provoked little more than incredulous stares. In 1840 he reasserted the usefulness of his newly coined term, but it enjoyed very little acceptance until almost 1900. Prior to that time there had always been a sharp distinction between knowledge and the knower. Whewell obliterated that distinction. He personified that which was not a person.

In 1874 Charles Hodge could still assert that "science, according to its etymology, is simply knowledge."[4] Hodge was talking of meaning shifts that had occurred particularly in England and the United States. The same, however, had not occurred in the German language, which retained the original, broader meaning of knowledge. Hodge went on to observe that in the German, the word *Wissenschaft* is used of all kinds of knowledge. In that historic German sense, all five of the professors at our table should have been called scientists, including the artist and the educator.

A second definition of science is closely harmonized with the first. Science is not merely knowledge but also the preserved collections of knowledge that have been categorized and classified as academic disciplines. Historically we have done this classifying and grouping according to the object or focal point of our study. In the twentieth century, however, there have been concerted efforts to classify knowledge according to the methodology of study, an approach that, says David Lindberg, "is fraught with all kinds of danger."[5] To claim that there is one category of knowledge that has exclusive right to the scientific or inductive approach, another that exclusively uses the rational or deductive approach, and still another that relies on faith is to admit a woeful ignorance of epistemology and to fabricate categories that are both false and fanciful.

When science is understood as either knowledge or a systematic arrangement of knowledge into categories, there is no reason to be afraid of science per se. But there is no reason to worship it either. For all of us, whether we are farmers or professors, bankers or housewives, biologists or musicians, to claim that we have a right to the scientific label and to be called scientists is then legitimate. Each of us may have some knowledge that the others do not possess, but all of us are woefully ignorant in areas where others shine. Not one of us can claim sole possession of science or superiority over the others, except in our narrow field of concentration. When such occurs, the luster and gloss of science will be gone, but that forebodes no tragic consequence for the intellectual marketplace.

Because of common usage, we can employ a third definition of science, namely, a method of study by which knowledge is acquired. When we think of science as a method of study, we are thinking of one of the ways by which all students and researchers work. It is frequently dubbed the inductive approach, whereby we proceed from specific cases to general conclusions. The most common label for this procedure is the scientific method. Everyone at our table that day rightly insisted and promptly illustrated that he or she used that method frequently.

When using the scientific method, the researcher proceeds through the following generally stated steps:

(a) formulation of a hypothesis or theory to be proven;
(b) selection of events or phenomena to be examined;
(c) observation and categorization of the selections;
(d) generalization from those observations to all other similar events and phenomena; and
(e) drawing conclusions and formulating laws on the basis of these observations.

Some people who make their living by doing research pretend that the scientific method is a highly complicated, narrow, technical activity. In one sense that is true, particularly if you are doing research on dangerous, explosive chemicals or on nuclear fission. In another sense, though, the method is as uncomplicated and common as counting yes and no answers to a simple question. In both examples people use the scientific method in essentially the same way. The only difference is that some scientists do their research with more potentially dangerous elements.

When science is understood in its classic, dictionary sense, there is no reason to fear it or worship it. Science cannot wage war against Christianity or, for that matter, do anything. It cannot send space capsules to the moon. It cannot date fossils. It cannot predict the weather. It cannot create new surgical techniques. It cannot prove the age of the earth. Science, above all, cannot prove any evolutionary theory to be true. Only human beings can attempt such things, but they can utilize the knowledge they have acquired in those efforts. As humans, they stand in allegiance either to the God of the universe or to the great satanic pretender to that throne. When they are in Satan's employ and then use all the science available to them, we better be on guard lest we come under his influence.

In many of our large cities we have a great deal of difficulty with street gangs. Usually composed of insecure adolescents or postadolescents, gangs make concerted and often dangerous efforts to protect their turf. A given neighborhood or area belongs to a particular gang and must be guarded against all intruders. Every gang has its unique symbols, signs, and permits for passage. If a rival gang so much as wears the wrong-colored shoelaces or dares to walk on the wrong side of an alley, its members run the risk of a gang war.

In many ways, the boundary disputes among scientists represent that same deep-seated insecurity and senseless need to protect their turf. Numerous theistic evolutionists bristle with emotion whenever someone from outside their close-knit group dares to challenge their scientific assertions. If that challenger is from the creationist camp, the epithets fly. "You are not a scientist" is the usual charge, followed by such characterizations as "dishonest," "biased," and "prejudiced." In addition to the blatantly unchristian character of such attacks, they display a deep-seated insecurity that calls into question the authenticity of their proponents' belief patterns.

Along with these patterns of insecurity, there are indicators of a false triumphalism. Just as each street gang claims to be in possession of great power, so the members of the natural sciences claim to be the queen of the sciences. Whereas theologians and philosophers had assumed that lofty seat during the late medieval era, now it is the biologists, chemists, astronomers, and geologists who pretend to have triumphed. As queens of academia, they can rewrite history, redefine the nature of man, and reinterpret the Scriptures. Traditional religious doctrines must be rejected, because new, scientific theories have been advanced. According to them, the first eleven chapters of Genesis may no longer be interpreted literally, because science has proved them to be mythological word pictures and prescientific fables.

If natural scientists would limit themselves to their own turf, as they deceptively claim to be doing, there would be less controversy, especially among Christians. But when they overstep their boundaries, turf wars erupt with expected and sometimes tragic consequences.

In trying to exclude all competitors or in trying to force all other disciplines into the mold of the natural sciences, certain presuppositions are almost always held, and assumptions made. These are not unique to natural scientists, but they are essential to the mode of operation used by the advocates of evolution.

Although there are numerous unproved assumptions on which evolutionary theory rests, one deserves special attention. It is the assumption that all of physical reality is and has always been orderly and consistent. Those who hold to it most tenaciously, however, prefer not to discuss it or even to acknowledge its existence, for it represents the Achilles' heel of scientism. Its most common name is uniformitarianism, representing a deep-seated belief in the uniformity of the laws of nature across time and space.

The concept of natural laws and their uniform application derives from the Age of Enlightenment and the mechanistic worldviews of the seventeenth and eighteenth centuries. Holding yet to a belief in God, the mechanists and their deist counterparts constructed the image of a universe elaborately designed and tuned so that it ran like a precision clock. In the process of postulating a wholly continuous, atomistic world of natural laws, immutably imbedded in nature, they changed our conception of not only nature but also nature's God. For the deists and those who continue in their train, God became a cosmic legislator, a grand governor, a deific designer, and a sustainer of the clockwork image. No longer was He the righteous and angry Creator who, in His righteous fury, upset the world with a cataclysmic flood. No longer was He Emmanuel, God with us, who intervened in nature for the sake of His people. No longer was He "our God" or "our Father" who disciplined His people because He loved them. On the contrary, He was merely the one who designed natural laws and set them in motion.

When Sir Charles Lyell published his *Principles of Geology* in 1830, the relevance of God to scientific activity had eroded even further. Since God was merely the clockmaker and the clock was the object of study, He could be conveniently ignored. The value of all scientific study, Lyell concluded, "must depend entirely on the degree of confidence which we feel in regard to the permanence of the laws of nature."[6] Some fifteen years later Louis Agassiz applied the same principle to his study of glaciers and then deduced, albeit illogically, that most of the northern hemisphere had for some time been covered with ice. A scant fifteen years further down the road, Charles Darwin utilized the same uniformitarian argument to develop *The Origin of Species*. He, like all uniformitarian scientists, worked "with observable, gradual, small-scale changes and extrapolated their effects through immense time to encompass the grand phenomena of history."[7]

There is something fascinating and believable about such a notion, such time-honored constancy and uniformity. A universe that presumably works in exactly the same way all the time is a source of comfort and confidence, especially when God is so far removed in His role as designer and observer. For those who practice scientism, the uniformity of the laws of nature becomes their cardinal principle of faith, quite unlike that of the Christian, who starts with "and God said."

The person who puts his trust in science and scientific progress displays "faith in the intrinsic goodness of human nature and in the omnipotence of science. It is a defiant and blasphemous faith, not unlike that held by the men who set out to build 'a city and a tower, whose top may reach unto heaven' and who believed that 'nothing will be restrained from them, which they have imagined to do.'"[8]

In one sense, it is depressing to come to the realization that science is no more powerful than a bag of sticks and stones. In a culture where scientism, or the worship of science, runs rampant, it is disconcerting to realize that one of our cultural idols has been reduced to the level of common knowledge. The hopes and dreams of a grand design are gone. Our idol has proved to be nothing more than a hollow, speechless, powerless idol. Of course that will make some people despondent.

But there is an alternative view. Knowledge and science are still legitimate. The words of Proverbs still stand: "Hold on to instruction, do not let it go; guard it well, for it is your life" (Prov. 4:13 NIV). Pursue knowledge, ask God for insight and understanding and wisdom, but in all your efforts, remember, "The fear of the LORD is the beginning of wisdom" (Prov. 9:10).

Knowledge is a gift from God. Because it is a gift, we must not worship it. Instead, we must give praise and thanks to the Giver, who alone is the Source of all knowledge, the only One who has all knowledge in His possession. When we worship the gift and ascribe power to it, we are guilty of scientism, which is a form of idolatry. When we see knowledge as a gift from God, we can direct all our worship to Him alone.

4 How Should We Understand Kids?

The sign outside the elementary classroom door was too big for anyone to miss. It read:

> Knowledge Available Here!
> Bring Your Own Container!

On first blush, this sign seemed clever. Children in this sixth-grade classroom could respond positively and have their heads filled with facts that the teacher thought to be important. The intent was to create excitement about the prospect of having one's brain filled with information. The hope was that kids would be motivated to learn and would come with anticipation of having their containers (i.e., their brains) filled to overflowing. Maybe, though, some cantankerous little characters would put the lid on and challenge the teacher to get something in over their resistance. Either way, there was the possibility of some exciting effort behind those classroom doors.

Down the street, at one of the village churches, the pastor conducted a catechism class. True to the catechetical tradition, the seasoned instructor prodded the students with numerous questions, hoping that he could extract from them the answers that he was seeking. Committed to the belief that children had the knowledge safely tucked away beneath their cranial cap, he tried to educate them, that is, to draw out that which they already had in possession. To teach was to lead out (*educere*) by properly phrased questions. When the pastor was not successful, he rephrased the question, because the fault as probably lay with the questioner as with the questioned.

Whenever philosophers or theorists attempt to understand and analyze the myriad of activities that make up the educational process, they inevitably try to reduce them to a basic model, pattern, or paradigm. When the specific subject is the character of the learning process or the nature of the educand (i.e., the dominant qualities of the learner), they quickly fall into a pattern that is often easily recognizable. Rather than get into a detailed discussion of all the unique and common characteristics of human beings, philosophers and psychologists quickly leave the details behind and go one of two ways. In the history of Western education two basic paradigms have dominated discussion. Almost all educational practice and methodology have been devised in response to one or the other of these models.

The Traditional Paradigms

The older of these two models is usually given the label of liberal arts or classical humanism. For decades, Christian colleges have been enamored with this tradition and have proudly called themselves liberal arts colleges. Translated, that means that they concentrate on the arts that liberate, or that free the person. In more recent years there has sprung up a movement among Christian elementary and secondary schools that has also embraced this paradigm. Called the classical school movement, it focuses its curriculum on the trivium and the quadrivium of the medieval era. Both of these movements claim to be Christian, but their roots are in a non-Christian paradigm.

One of the fundamental questions raised by learning theorists is whether knowledge has its origin or genesis in the mind or in the objects that make up our environment. For example, the question is whether the knowledge of a tree originates in the tree or in the mind of the person who observes the tree. Does the tree emit or radiate stimuli that bombard the senses and thus gain entrance into a passive receptacle called the mind, or does the mind actively search out the tree, make observations about it, and thus take to itself whatever is needed to understand the tree? In a classroom setting, the question is whether stimuli originate with the printed page or whether the mind extracts from the printed page those symbols which it then decodes into meaningful ideas. Put simply, the question is whether the mind is active or passive.

Whenever I would pose such questions to my students in educational psychology, they would tend to split their answers between the two options, with some of them either too timid or too wise to choose neither. Many of them wanted a quick and simple answer from me, so that they could quickly put it in their notebooks, memorize it for the next test, and get on with what they considered the real business of educating kids. They got nothing of the sort, however, for in the question as posed lies one of the major problems that have divided epistemologists since ancient times. In fact, I would warn them, the answer is neither, for the most essential element has been left out of the equation.

The genesis of this major debate, at least for the Western world, resides in the dialogues of Plato and has been nurtured through the ages by idealist philosophers such as Socrates, René Descartes, and Bishop George Berkeley and such gestaltists as Kurt Lewin, Edward C. Tolman, and Jean Piaget. The venerable Augustine can also be classified with this tradition, not because he was wedded to Platonic ideas but because he found much to be admired in the catechetical practices and tried to combine his Christian beliefs with Plato's idea of innate knowledge. As we shall see, the paradigm of innate knowledge is closer to the biblical model than is the empty-bucket model.

In numerous respects, the liberal arts approach to education and the cognitive approach to learning theory are rooted in the dialogues of Plato. The two dialogues that most cogently present Plato's theories are the *Phaedo* and the *Republic*. Particularly in the *Phaedo* we find that Plato's epistemology rests on the assertion that the soul preexisted in eternity and experienced an intimate relationship with the ultimate Good, or what he calls the Form. The soul, argues Plato, "is in the very likeness of the divine, and immortal, and rational, and uniform, and indissoluble, and unchangeable."[1] In contrast to the divine and immortal soul, "the body is in the very likeness of the human, and mortal, and irrational, and multiform, and dissoluble, and changeable."[2]

Through the dialectical argumentation of Socrates, Plato argues for absolute truth, residing ultimately beyond man, imbedded in eternity, and originated in the eternal Good.[3] Because the soul, which is seemingly equated with the mind, is coexistent with the Good in eternity, Plato asserts that man is born with innate ideas or latent knowledge. In trying to prove this essential point, he has Socrates arguing:

> Then before we began to see or hear or perceive in any way, we must have had a knowledge of absolute equality. . . . And if we acquired this knowledge before we were born, and were born having the use of it, then we also knew before we were born and at that instant of birth not only the equal or the greater or the less, but all other such ideas; for we are not speaking only of equality, but of beauty, goodness, justice, holiness, and of all which we stamp with the name of absolute being.[4]

For Plato, life after birth is not a matter of acquiring knowledge, but of forgetting and recollecting. Through his elaborate and sometimes almost facetious arguments, Plato asserts that the body with all of its sensory qualities is the prison house for the soul. The body, he says, is a hindrance, a deceiver of the soul, and offers, at best, inaccurate and indistinct witness to the eternal verities. Thought is best, Plato maintains,

> when the mind is gathered into herself—when she takes of the body, and has as little as possible to do with it, when she has no bodily sense or desire. . . . He attains to the purest knowledge of them who goes to each with the intellect alone, not introducing or intruding in the act of thought, sight, or any other sense . . . he who has got rid, as far as he can, of eyes and ears and, so to speak, of the whole body.[5]

The body must give up its claims if the person is to be restored to a perfect state. As the child leaves the birth canal, he[6] has all knowledge within his being, but that knowledge remains trapped inside the body until someone can skillfully draw it out. According to Plato, learning is the discovery of internalized truths as latent ideas are brought to consciousness. Education is not the acquiring of new knowledge but the recalling of that which is already known. In the *Phaedo* he presses the point:

> Your favorite doctrine . . . that our learning is simply recollection, if true, also necessarily implies a previous time in which we have learned that which we now recollect.[7]

The primary tool for such recollection or elucidation is the dialectical or catechetical method, more simply known as questioning. Nowhere is it more skillfully demonstrated than by Plato and Socrates in the dialogues, all of which employ the method and pry out the most stubborn answers by skillful questioning. In the words of Socrates, the teacher is not to function as a dispenser of information but as a midwife, assisting in the delivery process.

Not everyone in Athens was willing to concede the point to Plato. One of his most famous students, none other than Aristotle, raised a serious objection. In his *Nicomachean Ethics* Aristotle argued,

> The faculties given us by nature are bestowed on us first in a potential form; we exhibit their actual exercise afterward. . . . Because we had the senses we began to use them; we did not get them by using them.[8]

Aristotle was willing to concede that the child had potential for acquiring ideas, but he would not grant that they were present at birth. Through the senses, from outside the body, came the information, the ideas, the knowledge that might find a home within the soul but did not originate there. In fact, he argued, there is not even good evidence for the existence of a soul, for man is best characterized as being a rational animal, at the apex of the animal family but not in the distinct category of human. (Note the precursor to Darwin's evolutionary theory.) Aristotle's theory of potentiality quickly gained influential followers and advocates, none more powerful than Thomas Aquinas, who put Aristotle on a par with the author of the Bible. Treating the Word of God as no more authoritative than Aristotle's works, the most prestigious thinker of the Middle Ages pushed forward the concept that the child comes into the world analogous to an empty bucket that must be filled through the avenue of the senses.

The great debate between these two paradigms accelerated during the Age of Enlightenment, led by such influential thinkers as Ignatius of Loyola, Jean Jacques Rousseau, Jan Amos Comenius, Johann Heinrich Pestalozzi, and Johann Friedrich Herbart. Key to the debate was a theoretical question originally posed by John Locke. Musing on the matter, he asked,

> Let us suppose the mind to be, as we say, white paper, void of all characters, without any ideas, how comes it to be furnished? Whence has it all the materials of reason and knowledge? To this I answer, in one word, From experience; in that all our knowledge is founded, and from that it ultimately derives itself.[9]

Notice that Locke did not assert that the mind was a blank slate but hypothetically asked, if it were, how then would the mind become filled? The question was initially construed as a possible hypothesis, not as an irrefutable fact. Locke's "white paper," however, was thenceforth pictured as a tabula rasa, or blank slate, on which nothing was written until after the child had left the womb. Then, through the senses of seeing, hearing, touching, tasting, and smelling, the child would gradually come to knowledge about the world around him, beginning with his immediate environment and then slowly expanding to worlds more abstract and distant.

Since Locke's time, the vast majority of educational leaders came to embrace this paradigm. Men like John Dewey, Ivan Pavlov, Immanuel Kant, Jean Piaget, B. F. Skinner, John Watson, and a host of others have come to embrace the tabula rasa model. The child is innocent at birth, they have all asserted, because there is nothing there to have been corrupted. The child is not born evil; he becomes evil. The child becomes evil only as he grows older and as he is influenced by a corrupt environment. In such a model there is no room for original sin or total depravity, although increasing and deadly amounts of corruption may creep in from the outside. In the latter half of the twentieth century, especially in North America, it is difficult to find a college of education that will give serious consideration to the Platonic paradigm and even contemplate the question of innate knowledge. Books on educational psychology are often written without so much as a mention of Plato or his dialogues. Schools, at least in the public sector, have embraced Locke's model.

Millions of educators in America have bought into this rather silly and badly distorted notion. Education, in such a perspective, is a simple, shallow kind of endeavor with no room allowed for discernment between truth and falsehood, no room for character development, and no room for spiritual nourishment. Religion thus is a manmade product designed to explain evil and find a way out of it. Moral training is not even to be considered, for it is nothing more than a phase of socialization, with each society setting its own standards for what it conceives morality to be. There is no right or wrong, for there is no absolute truth or righteousness. Education in such a milieu is a process of filling sterile brains with facts. Add to that some discussion about training of skills, and our agenda will be full.

Both of these paradigms are fundamentally faulty. Neither one comports well with reality, and neither is based on the authoritative Word of the God who has created all persons. Both the fill-'em-up and the draw-'em-out models are false, for both fail to capture the complexity and the mystery of the human soul. In the pages ahead we will try to capture some of that complexity, some of what it means to be fearfully and wonderfully made in the image of our Creator.

The Transformational Paradigm

We have argued that neither Plato's nor Aristotle's models for man will stand the test of careful scriptural reading. Nowhere in the pages of Holy Writ will one find support for the notion that man is omniscient from the moment of birth or for the notion that the child is ignorant at birth. The truth lies somewhere in between and must be expressed in some other form.

At the risk of offending some non-Reformed friends, let me call it the reforming or the transformational model. Both words are appropriate, and both are necessary to carry the freight that the paradigm conveys. Let me begin to explain the meaning of reforming Christian education by illustration from an administrators' conference that I attended ten years ago, when a large gathering of Christian school principals and superintendents met at Disney World near Orlando, Florida. In an unusual program arrangement, we participated in a Walt Disney World seminar production entitled "Promoting Excellence in Your School." For the better part of three days we studied and listened in the luxury of a Disney World hotel. The seminar leaders were skilled, polished, and professional. The package they presented was honed, sharpened, and sweetened by the best marketing agents Disney could find.

If the Platonic paradigm had been employed, the seminar leaders should have concentrated primarily on drawing our innate marketing strategies out of our sin-encrusted psyches. If the Aristotelian or Lockean model had been correct, they should have stuffed our heads with new information and created an environment for absorption.

But something else was going on, and most of the Christian school leaders sensed it. A skillfully conceived competitive game was being played. There were two kingdoms in competition, the kingdom of Christ and the magic kingdom of Walt Disney. There was the overt and presumably neutral marketing strategy that could be applied to any kingdom enterprise, but it was always coated in the language and imagery of Walt Disney's world.

As the sessions wore on, it was somewhat refreshing and almost a bit embarrassing to hear the critique of the program. These Christian school leaders intuitively knew that they had to critique the culture in which they were being enmeshed and squeezed against the Word of God. Silently they asked such questions as Is the magic kingdom a religious kingdom? Who is king in Walt Disney's world? What is the primary mission of the magic kingdom? Is the magic kingdom in conflict with the kingdom of God? Are they wholly incompatible? Or can I straddle the fence and enjoy the pleasures of both with offense to neither?

Bible-believing Christians who live out of the Word know that the world is a hostile place and not a friend to God. They know that both evil and good exist. They know that they are responsible for making judgments about whatever they encounter. They have to choose for good and against evil. They have consciences. They are born with an innate sense of right and wrong. Even the littlest child knows the difference. But then they stroll those palm-shaded streets of fake castles, clean fun, and forever smiling characters who either sell their soul to Disney or get fired on the thinnest pretense. Cavorting through such an environment seems sheer pleasure to some. For the concerned Christian, however, it is an experience that requires care, caution, and critical discernment. What we have in Disney World is not an innocent, purely pleasurable place for escape from the world but a highly tantalizing temptation to love the world.

We in the reforming tradition have often summarized the teaching of Scripture around the creation-fall-redemption theme. In the context of the Heidelberg Catechism we also describe it as the sin-salvation-service motif. In summary it is this:

1. A perfect, sovereign God created Adam and Eve as good, righteous, wise, and holy images of Himself.
2. Through their own will and the enticement of Satan, Adam and Eve disobeyed God and became darkened in their minds, perverse in their judgments, and impure in their affections (Canons of Dort, third and fourth head of doctrine).
3. Through the daily operation of the Holy Spirit and the perfect obedience of Jesus Christ, the descendants of Adam and Eve can be restored to the perfect state enjoyed in Eden.

That sounds familiar and probably comes across as overly simplified. It is. This redemption or restoration process is no simple experience and not without its complicating factors. The work of the Holy Spirit is described as irresistible because of the innate resistance and the external forces competing against Him. In diagram form we have a situation that looks like that in figure 1.

Fig. 1. Three Possible Responses to the Fall

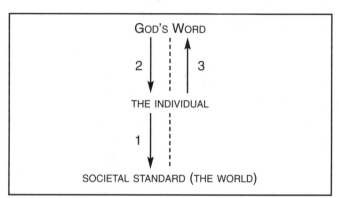

The three factors are pictured in this higher-to-lower relationship to illustrate the fall of man. God's Word represents the normative standard for all of life. Because of sin, man fell from grace. He hangs not in a vacuum but in a constant tension between the demands of a righteous God and the allurements of a seductive world. One of the most profound and most important questions that man can ever address is that of his response to his fallen predicament. Let me suggest three possible answers:

1. He can quietly conform to worldly standards and submit to the siren songs of society.
2. He can try to drag God's Word down to his level so that he is no longer at odds with it. This requires that he reinterpret or reexplain or delete offensive parts of God's Word so as to make it conform to his way of thinking. Thomas Jefferson attempted this by deleting vast sections of the Bible that ascribed too much authority to Christ and that preferred the kingdom over his vision of a democracy. Many feminists are attempting the same thing by trying to have the Bible rewritten in their own gender-neutral terms.
3. The third alternative is to stop fighting, become submissive, and allow ourselves to be "transformed by the renewing of [our] mind[s]," which is our spiritual worship, holy and pleasing to God (Rom. 12:1–2).

As redeemed and adopted children of God, we know very well that we may not conform any longer to the pattern of this world. We know too that it is equally wrong to try to drag God's normative standard down to our perverted level. Our only recourse is to become reformed, to be made over, to submit to the irresistible power of the Spirit and allow Him to reshape and remake us in our Father's image.

To be reformed is then to be ever reforming. That is the essence of the Reformed paradigm in education, but it is also one source of mass confusion and widespread disagreement. What or who must be reformed? What must be preserved intact? Where may change not intrude?

What must be changed is ourselves. What must be preserved intact is God's Word to us. In some ways that is a dangerous and tricky business, with thousands of pitfalls along the way. Naturally we resist when someone comes along and tells us we have to change. Naturally we rebel when parents, teachers, or pastors come with all their persuasive powers and coerce us to reform our perspectives, reshape our values, or remake our behavior patterns.

When those demands and pressures come, the most natural response is resistance, fueled by the intense power of Satan, who wants to claim our allegiance for himself. What God designs for good, the devil tries to distort for evil. When God wants us to comply, Satan wants us to rebel.

We are called to be reformed not in a neutral, idyllic peace garden but in the midst of a hostile world, a competitive and conflicting environment. Caught in the crunch of the great antithesis between the sovereign Lord of the universe and the great pretender to His throne, we are called to repent, to change our minds from what is wrong to what is right.

That is what was going on those days when hundreds of Christian school administrators sat in Orlando trying to market the message of Christ's kingdom while being tempted by the magic kingdom. What appeared sweet and innocent on the surface proved to be something quite different when viewed from the inside. Once we had taken our backstage, inside-the-organization tours, we saw much more clearly what was right and what was wrong. Against the floodlight of His Word, we knew that we could not serve both God and pleasure. With varying degrees of clarity, we heard the message: "Do not conform any longer to the pattern of this world, but be transformed by the renewing of your mind. Then you will be able to test and approve what God's will is—[H]is good, pleasing and perfect will!" (Rom. 12:1–2 NIV).

What went on in Orlando is a picture of what goes on every day in our Christian homes, churches, and schools. We are caught, pulled, tugged, and torn between the competing powers of this world. We want to be good, yet we are inclined to evil. We love the Lord, yet we listen to Satan. We know what is right, yet we do the wrong.

Christian education isn't easy. It isn't all joy and peace. It never was, and it never will be, at least not in this life. To reform a person from what he is to what he ought to be requires pain, patience, and perseverance. But to be co-workers with God in that great process of sanctification whereby we are, by the power of the Holy Spirit, slowly, gradually being restored to that state of perfection is also to experience some of the greatest rewards and joys that can ever be imagined. To influence the lives of others for good is what makes teaching worth all the frustrations that so often seem to cloud it.[10]

5   How Corrupt Are We?

But are we so corrupt that we are wholly incapable of doing any good, and inclined to all evil? (Heidelberg Catechism, Lord's Day 3, question 8)

I could hardly believe my eyes. There on the front page of the *Chicago Tribune* was a picture of a teacher in one of the Chicago public elementary schools handing out wads of toilet paper to boys and girls who were lined up, waiting their turn to go to the bathroom. These students were not given rolls of paper but carefully doled out numbers of sheets peeled off a roll in the teacher's hands. In the bathrooms, the article said, there were no soap dispensers, no paper towels, no hand dryers, and no toilet paper. Because some pupils have kicked them down, there are no doors on some stalls. Because some pupils have ripped them from the walls, there are no soap dispensers at the sinks.

And yet the situation in that southern part of Chicago was no different from one at the Christian school in Rock Valley, Iowa, fifty years ago when I was growing up. We had the same procedures at our four-room school for a number of years, because we were no better. This kind of behavior is not endemic to inner-city people but is characteristic of all men everywhere until they have been transformed by the power of the Holy Spirit.

In another incident, so typical of what goes on in elementary and secondary schools, three twelve-year-old girls pleaded guilty to charges of aggravated battery for lacing their teachers' coffee and soft drinks with laxatives. The prank sent three teachers and a student teacher to the hospital, where all were treated and released. Having served as a school administrator for ten years, I know that such actions are not all that rare. Students often become angry and frustrated with their teachers, their parents, and their peers. For teachers to be threatened with bodily harm is not unusual, even in elementary schools, where kindergarten kids will throw temper tantrums and assault those who are called to teach them. Many larger schools in our bigger cities find it necessary to employ police patrols in their hallways and to set up metal detectors at their outside doors. In one large public high school that I visited occasionally, the entire ground floor was equipped with bulletproof glass. Even with such security measures in place, bomb threats are becoming commonplace and gang warfare is a frequent occurrence.

In the world of education and child welfare, large numbers of people continue to insist that none of us are innately bad but that we merely engage in learned behavior. These are the same people who never want to blame children for their misdeeds but blame instead the environment in which the children have been reared. They claim that children do evil or wrong things only because they are imitating the behaviors around them. They insist that children who grow up in the slums, or the projects, as Chicagoans now call them, have no chance to become good citizens because they see only bad behavior around them. They learn strictly by imitation and not by natural inclination.

People who hold this view keep clamoring for more money for inner-city schools so that they can change the environment, so that they can rebuild people's lives. The source of the problem, they contend, is the environment around the person and not the person himself. These people would be terribly offended by the practice of handing out small amounts of toilet paper in public school hallways. Presumably such disciplinary measures would erode the already poor self-images of these innocent victims.

The Antidote from Scripture

A good antidote to the perspective of our liberal news media is that afforded us on the pages of Scriptures. The apostle Peter's letters were written during the time of Nero, when Christians were being severely persecuted. These letters have been described as being "epistles to pilgrims in pagan lands." Peter argues that the culture in which he and his readers were living can only be described as being both pagan and profoundly corrupt. In one chapter Peter warns that there have been and will be false teachers who will deliberately try to destroy the truth. They will persistently, glibly, and effectively tell falsehoods as a matter of regular practice. Peter says, "They will secretly introduce destructive heresies . . . bringing swift destruction on themselves" (2 Peter 2:1 NIV). These persons will be effective, for "many will follow their shameful ways and will bring the way of truth into disrepute" (v. 2 NIV).

Peter goes on to say of these people that they "follow the corrupt desire of the sinful nature and despise authority. Bold and arrogant . . . , they are like brute beasts, creatures of instinct, born only to be caught and destroyed" (vv. 10–12 NIV). "They are blots and blemishes, reveling in their pleasures. . . . With eyes full of adultery, they never stop sinning; they seduce the unstable; they are experts in greed—an accursed brood" (vv. 13–14 NIV). Peter makes a point of setting up two prime examples of how bad it has been at some points in history. He first points to the time of Noah and the flood, when the world became so evil, and when sin was so rampant and so widespread that God would not tolerate it any longer. We are told in Genesis that "the LORD saw how great man's wickedness on the earth had become, and that every inclination of the thoughts of his heart was only evil all the time" (Gen. 6:5 NIV). Every family except one, that of Noah and his three sons, had sunk to such low levels of evil and wickedness that God "was grieved that [H]e had made man on the earth, and [H]is heart was filled with pain" (Gen. 6:6 NIV). The vast majority of people, including men and women and children, were practicing such wholesale, persistent evil that God ran out of patience with them. In His anger, God saw fit to destroy them all, except Noah's family.

The other example that Peter brings to the attention of his readers is the situation with Sodom and Gomorrah. By citing the sins of Sodom, he reminds us that Lot, "a righteous man, . . . was distressed . . . by the lawless deeds he saw and heard" (2 Peter 2:7–8 NIV), and thereby Peter calls attention to the sins of homosexuality and lesbianism as some of the most vile, gross, despicable sins practiced by mankind. In the Greek, Peter writes chiefly about "those who walk according to the flesh in the lust of uncleanness and despise authority" (v. 10).

Peter makes it plain to his readers that God will not tolerate evil. God is righteous and holy and will not look the other way when His creatures sin against Him and when they break any of His laws. In his comments about the false teachers who are going to secretly introduce destructive heresies, Peter states that God will bring judgment and justice. God will not leave sin unpunished. Peter reminds his readers that "their condemnation has long been hanging over them, and their destruction has not been sleeping" (v. 3 NIV). To make his point, Peter tells them that God "did not spare angels . . . , but sent them to hell" (v. 4 NIV). We can assume that these would be Satan and his followers, who rebelled against God in heaven, presumably some time before Satan came to earth to tempt Eve and Adam. Without going into detail, Peter tells us that God "put them into gloomy dungeons to be held for judgment" (v. 4). Peter also reminds us that God had been so angry with the people whom He had created that He regretted that He had ever made them. In His anger He literally wiped almost every one of them from off the face of the earth. The flood was so catastrophic that only those who were in the ark survived.

The third example that Peter uses to illustrate God's response to evil is that carried out against Sodom and Gomorrah during the time of Lot. God was so incensed at the rampant evil, and particularly at the homosexual behavior of the men, that "he condemned the cities of Sodom and Gomorrah by burning them to ashes." Peter goes on to tell us that God "made them an example of what is going to happen to the ungodly" (v. 6 NIV). To send fire and brimstone out of the sky and to use that to burn two cities with all of their inhabitants is an indication of the tremendous anger that God has against sin.

When Paul addresses this question, he says that God "will punish those who do not know God and do not obey the gospel of the Lord Jesus. They will be punished with everlasting destruction and shut out from the presence of the Lord" (2 Thess. 1:8–9 NIV).

In the book of Revelation we read that the devil will be cast into the lake of fire and brimstone, where also the beast and the false prophet had been thrown. "They will be tormented day and night, for ever and ever" (Rev. 20:10 NIV).

Some readers might be inclined to think that such wholesale manifestation of evil is confined to an earlier era, a time before men became civilized and respectful of one another. Such idealistic thinking is true of those who embrace the theory of social Darwinism, but it has no basis in reality. One has only to read the daily newspapers for a short time to accumulate a wealth of articles certifying the hateful attitudes of even the youngest children. A few days of reading will remind you of wholesale demonstrations in our society. Pornography is available in our movie theaters or in our magazines. The drug culture thrives among both the wealthy and the poor, in the heart of ghettos but also with increasing incidence in farm villages and quiet, affluent suburbs. Vulgar language has become acceptable in some of our schools. Illicit sex outside of marriage is commonplace, as is bribery in government and in the police departments. Shameless tabloids line almost every grocery checkout lane in the United States. People are slaughtered by the hundreds of thousands in countries like the Sudan, Bosnia, Zaire, and Rwanda, as they were in Nazi Germany, or in Rome during the time of Nero and others. Christians are persecuted in communist China and in southern Sudan, to cite two examples.

Man is incurably wicked.

One night a few years ago, a television reporter interviewed a class of elementary students concerning their feelings about Dennis Rodman's suspension from the Chicago Bulls basketball team. All of the students except for one boy wanted to see Rodman back on the basketball court as soon as possible. They saw nothing offensive or evil about his behavior. They truly liked what they saw. That is probably true of the majority of the people in this country, who keep buying his book, his shirts, his pictures, his cards, and whatever else he happens to be selling. What is so frightening is that the majority of children and their parents seem to find nothing repulsive about this character or others like him. They love him because through him they can do exactly what they want; they can sin vicariously and not experience any of the consequences, at least not immediately. But there will come a day. God is not mocked; He will execute judgment on all who have it coming.

This particular individual has lived and boasted about an obviously immoral lifestyle. He loves to remind everyone that he is *As Bad as I Want to Be*, the title of his book. He seems to have no fear of any punishment and seems to delight in getting kicked out of ball games and out of bars, because that makes him more outrageous, and therefore more popular, and therefore wealthier. He seems to have no fear of God in his heart. He confuses God's lack of punishment at this point with permission. He confuses divine patience with approval. Peter's assessment that "for a long time their judgment has not been idle, and their destruction does not slumber" (2 Peter 2:3) would apply to this former member of the Bulls.

Why don't more people use illegal drugs? Why don't more men beat their wives? Why don't more children steal from the candy store? Why don't more people drive ninety miles an hour on the freeway? Why don't more teenagers blow through stop signs? Why don't more people buy more pornographic magazines? Because God has surrounded us with restraining forces that keep on saying that all of these things are wrong, they are evil, and they will result in punishment if we should ever be caught doing them. That restraint comes through the government that God has instituted and established so that "whoever resists the authority resists the ordinance of God, and those who resist will bring judgment on themselves" (Rom. 13:2). We need governments to hold in check the natural evil that characterizes all of us. We need laws and police and the Federal Bureau of Investigation and the news media to expose and restrain the evil that is so natural to us all.

Our children would watch garbage on their computer screens and on television if they had no one to scold or punish them. Our sons and daughters would use offensive language if they thought either that they would not be caught or that they would not be punished. Only because they have parents and siblings who care enough to say no and only because the Holy Spirit restrains sin in their lives do they stay away from evil. Not only parents but also brothers and sisters, cousins and grandparents, neighbors and friends serve as restraining influences on us, keeping us from doing the kinds of sins we would do if they were not there. Teachers and bus drivers, along with all responsible adults, help to keep our children from acting out what is natural to them.

All of these forces are helpful in the restraint of sin, but they never can cure the root cause. Sin is original with us. It comes from our heart. Like a crack cocaine baby, we are born with an addiction to sin. Even if we built walls one hundred feet high around us, we would still be prone by nature to engage in all kinds of wickedness. Peter reminds us that God is not only a God of justice and wrath but also a compassionate God who rescues His people and keeps them from destruction. Though God did not spare the world from the ravages of the flood, He also "protected Noah, a preacher of righteousness, and seven others" (2 Peter 2:5 NIV).

Peter also reminds us of divine compassion in the story of Sodom and Gomorrah, telling us that God condemned the cities of Sodom and Gomorrah but "delivered righteous Lot, who was oppressed by the filthy conduct of the wicked" (v. 7). Best of all, we need to remember the lesson in Paul's letter to the Ephesians. Through no merit of our own, through no acts of ours, God chose us "before the creation of the world" to be elected by Him and to be made holy and blameless before Him in Christ. God could have left all of us in our sinful condition and allowed us to go on sinning until we had destroyed ourselves, until we would rot forever in the fires of hell; but He chose us to be saved, to be rescued from sin, just as He chose Noah and his family to be saved by the ark, just as He chose Lot to be spared from the fires of Sodom and Gomorrah, and just as He chose Rahab to be spared from the destruction of Jericho.

The picture of man thus far portrayed is dark and ominous. If total depravity and original sin were the only things we could find to describe the students we are called to educate, the picture would be enough to keep all except the bravest out of the classroom. If the whole tale has been told, there would never be any joy in Mudville High or delight in Kankakee Kindergarten.

There is more to the story than this dark, foreboding side, for God's Word also tells us that He made all of us in His image and endowed every one of us with wonderful gifts and talents.

Made in His Image?

Some teachers approach the classroom as though every child in it were the embodiment of Satan. "The little devils" is an oft-heard remark coming from their lips. It reminds me of a long-time friend who served as principal of a junior high school near our home. Noted for the strict discipline code he enforced at his school, he often remarked, "The little squirrels are up to it again!" A thoroughgoing evolutionist, he could not think of his charges in human terms but always had to label them as crafty little animals. Others in the profession approach the classroom as though the children in it were a host of angels, with nary a smirch on their wings of pearly white.

There are times when each of the preceding designations might seem appropriate. But all of them miss some important truths about the persons that God has brought into existence. No one is so corrupt or wicked that he deserves to be labeled as absolutely depraved or to be equated with the devil. Absolute depravity means that a person is as bad as he could possibly be. That is not what the Bible teaches. Total depravity, though, is an accurate description of mankind because it rightly conveys the truth that the total range of man's being has been affected by sin. No part of the person, whether that is his will, his intellect, his emotion, his reasoning, or his gifts, has escaped the curse of sin. Every part, because of that curse, is now adversely affected and functions imperfectly. His will is imperfect. His reasoning is imperfect. His memory is imperfect. His ability to discern is imperfect. His ability to love his neighbor is imperfect. His ability to obey His God and those placed in authority is imperfect. Every part of him is flawed, but every part still functions.

When God created Adam and Eve, He created them in His likeness, in His image (Gen. 1:26–27). To be created in the image of God is a tremendous blessing that was not erased by Adam and Eve's fall into sin. That means that we were originally created with power, with the ability to rule, with the ability to understand our world clearly, and with the ability to live in a righteous relationship with each other and with God. Man was created to live in harmony, in peace, in holiness, and in truth. Man was created with a free will, by which he could make right choices or wrong ones. He was created as a free, moral agent who knew right from wrong.

In the greatest failure in human history, Adam and Eve together made a wrong choice. Instead of following the simple command of God and living in obedience to Him, they listened to the siren song of Satan and followed his clever distortion. The consequences were just as God had promised. Instead of living forever, they were enticed by falsehood and chose the way of death. Because of that disobedience, God said to Eve,

> I will greatly multiply your sorrow and your conception;
> In pain you shall bring forth children;
> Your desire shall be for your husband,
> And he shall rule over you. (Gen. 3:16)

To Adam He said,

> Cursed is the ground for your sake;
> In toil you shall eat of it
> All the days of your life.
> Both thorns and thistles it shall bring forth for you,
> And you shall eat the herb of the field.
> In the sweat of your face you shall eat bread
> Till you return to the ground,
> For out of it you were taken;
> For dust you are,
> And to dust you shall return. (vv. 17–19)

The consequences of their action were huge. Instead of enjoying the freedom of their original wills, they became estranged from God and hid from His sight. Instead of functioning perfectly, they suffered the distortions that came with the curse, for now they would return to the earth from which they had come. Instead of living in obedient service to their Creator, ruling over the creation as God had intended, they were driven out of the garden and forced to fight the thorns and thistles that grew everywhere.

The image of God was not taken away, but it was radically affected by the curse. Now, instead of living in peace with each other and with God, their relationships were soured, their hearts were filled with fear, their vision was impaired, and their work was always imperfect. It wasn't long before their sons got into a serious fight, with Cain killing his brother Abel. Living in fear, the murderer pleaded with God, "My punishment is greater than I can bear! Surely You have driven me out this day from the face of the ground; I shall be hidden from Your face; I shall be a fugitive and a vagabond on the earth, and it will happen that anyone who finds me will kill me" (Gen. 4:13–14).

The consequences of their sin notwithstanding, every descendant of Adam and Eve is still created in the image of God. Every child who enters a classroom, no matter how naughty and hateful he might be, is still made in the image of his Maker. As a young child bears a resemblance to his father, so children bear a resemblance to the divine. In a fashion that goes beyond human comprehension, every child is born with a conscience, an innate sense of right and wrong. Jesus Himself addressed the matter when He confronted the scribes and Pharisees who had brought before Him the woman caught in the act of adultery. As a perfect rebuttal to their devious efforts to trap Him, Jesus appealed to their consciences by saying, "He who is without sin among you, let him throw a stone at her first" (John 8:7). Then those who heard it, "being convicted by their conscience, went out one by one" (John 8:8).

The apostle Paul, in his defense before Felix, appealed to the governor's sense of justice by pleading, "I myself always strive to have a conscience without offense toward God and men" (Acts 24:16). In his letter to the Romans, Paul reminds his readers that all men tend to "suppress the truth in unrighteousness, because what may be known of God is manifest in them, for God has shown it to them" (Rom. 1:18–19).

What Plato had labeled as innate knowledge of eternal Forms is better described as an innate knowledge of what is right and what is wrong. "Conscience" means "with knowledge." In some miraculous way, beyond our wildest imaginations, God has somehow endowed every child, no matter how evil his parents might have become, with a knowledge of what is right and what is wrong. Any gynecologist or any pediatrician or any clinical psychologist who pretends to comprehend that miracle of birth, who pretends to explain that incomprehensible endowment, is fooling himself, for it defies every biological and physiological explanation known to man. Yet that knowledge is there for every observant parent and every teacher to behold. You accept it, you believe it, you observe it, but you cannot explain it.

The conscience can be seared, and the knowledge of what is right can be suppressed, smothered, and quenched, but it cannot be eradicated.

> God will not allow human beings to suppress entirely their sense of God and of His judgment. Some sense of right and wrong, as well as of accountability to God, always remains. Even in the fallen world, everyone is endowed with a conscience that from time to time condemns them, telling them that they ought to suffer for wrongs they have done. When conscience speaks in these terms, it speaks with the voice of God."[1]

In Platonic terms, knowing what *is* was judged of great significance. In biblical terms, however, knowing what *is right* and what *is wrong* is of far greater importance. Far from being the hypothetical object of rational conjecture that characterized Plato's theory of innate knowledge, the conscience is explained by God Himself, who speaks of the matter numerous times in the New Testament (Rom. 9:1; 13:5; 1 Cor. 10:25; 1 Tim. 3:9; 4:2; Heb. 9:14; 10:22; 1 Peter 3:16). In the words of Jeremiah's marvelous prophecy, God has promised, "I will put My law in their minds, and write it on their hearts; and I will be their God, and they shall be My people. No more shall every man teach his neighbor, and every man his brother, saying, 'Know the LORD,' for they shall all know Me, from the least of them to the greatest of them" (Jer. 31:33–34).

Those who remember the truths about the image of God can find real joy in the classroom. Just knowing that these kids, whose behavior sometimes can be so offensive, are created in the image of God Himself is a wonderful consolation. To help those children come to grips with the awesome character of their personal creation, to catch a vision of what God has given them, is excitement of the highest order. Without getting distorted by the muddled theology of New Age religion, we know that our body is "the temple of the Holy Spirit who is in you, whom you have from God" (1 Cor. 6:19). God the Holy Spirit lives in us and has given to all of us wonderful gifts that need to be developed for His honor and glory. Paul expresses those truths so succinctly when he writes, "He Himself gave some to be apostles, some prophets, some evangelists, and some pastors and teachers, for the equipping of the saints, for the work of ministry, for the edifying of the body of Christ" (Eph. 4:11–12).

Lest we falsely conclude that only spiritual gifts of ministry are provided directly by God, we need to turn also to the book of Exodus. There God speaks directly to Moses and informs him, "See, I have called by name Bezaleel. . . . And I have filled him with the Spirit of God, in wisdom, in understanding, in knowledge, and in all manner of workmanship, to design artistic works, to work in gold, in silver, in bronze, in cutting jewels for setting, in carving wood, and to work in all manner of workmanship" (Ex. 31:2–5). Then God tells Moses, "Indeed, I have appointed with him Aholiab. . . . And I have put wisdom in the hearts of all the gifted artisans, that they may make all that I have commanded you, the tabernacle of meeting, the ark of the Testimony and the mercy seat that is on it" (vv. 6–7).

To contemplate the mechanics of such endowment and such live-in presence of the divine is excitement of the first order. Then, to help those students identify and polish those gifts is the source of tremendous joy and satisfaction. To counterbalance the wonders of being made in the image of God with the truths of total depravity is to ensure a healthy dose of realism blanketed by a layer of almost rapture. Yes, our children come into the world affected by original sin, but they also are made "a little lower than the angels, and You have crowned [them] with glory and honor" (Ps. 8:5).

Greetings to the Saints

Every morning, all across the land, school buses and car pools drop off young children at schoolhouse doors, some at unearthly hours, before the sun has even peeked over the horizon. If the school is well run, the teachers are waiting to greet their charges with a cheery good morning. If it isn't the first day of a new year, those teachers ought to know all of the children by name and welcome them personally, happily saying, "Good morning, Craig! Good morning, Ana! Good morning, Ian!"

Such a welcome would help to start the day on a positive note and bring at least a faint smile to those who didn't enjoy the bus ride or didn't get enough sleep. If the teacher is genuine in her bright and sunny disposition, at least the first hour of the day should have a chance of being pleasant. Maybe no one will defy her until after the morning recess break, when it becomes apparent that the math assignment was not finished.

But suppose, for a moment, that Mr. Betten, a caring and insightful teacher, greeted those same youngsters with a cheery, "Good morning, Saint Craig! Good morning, Saint Ana! Good morning, Saint Ian!" Would those students respond with, "Good morning, Saint Betten!" or would they stop in stunned disbelief and think that the good teacher has had his marbles rattled and needs attention quickly? Would they believe their ears, or would they wonder about this teacher's off-the-wall humor?

We have been so conditioned in our Western culture that we would not be ready or willing to take such greeting at face value. Saints are few and far between. Only the greatest Christians that have ever lived deserve such acclaim. Saint Augustine, yes; Saint Peter, yes; Saint Francis, probably. But Saint Craig? No! Furthermore, no saints are living, for it is prerequisite that you have died before you could ever be elevated to sainthood. Also, it is clearly understood that no lowly elementary teacher has the right of designating who deserves to be addressed as saint. Only the pope, after years of consideration and examination of the evidence, could label any believer with such a glorious title.

The Roman Catholic, the Greek Orthodox, the Russian Orthodox, the Anglican, and the Episcopal churches have cornered that market for millennia. It is best that no second-grade teacher take it upon himself to proclaim any student in his class to be a saint. Maybe Mother Teresa will be the next to reach that lofty level, maybe even before the normal waiting period is up, but not Craig, or Ana, or Gracie, or Bradley.

But maybe we have been duped for a long time. Maybe we have not been reading our Bibles enough, and maybe we have not adequately reflected on what is said there. Did not the apostle Paul write to the church at Ephesus: "To the saints who are in Ephesus, and faithful in Christ Jesus" (Eph. 1:2)? Had he not served that church for only three years before he left for another charge (Acts 20:30)? How could he know them so well as to declare any of them saints? Furthermore, were not these folks in the church at Ephesus a rather sorry, unruly lot? Were they not so ignorant that they had to be taught the most elementary knowledge about the Holy Spirit (Acts 19:2)? Had not most of these people invested heavily in books of magic and sorcery, having to destroy a stockpile valued at fifty thousand pieces of silver (Acts 19:19)? Did not Paul have to warn their elders that "from among yourselves men will rise up, speaking perverse things, to draw away the disciples after themselves" (Acts 20:30)? How could Paul make such a blunder?

If Paul did indeed make such a blunder, he made it more than once and repeated it in a number of places. When he later wrote his letter to the church at Rome, he addressed it "to all who are in Rome, beloved of God, called to be saints" (Rom 1:7). When writing to the church members at Corinth, he addressed his letter "to those who are sanctified in Christ Jesus, called to be saints, with all who in every place call on the name of Jesus Christ our Lord" (1 Cor. 1:2). Very conscious of that church's shortcomings and demonstrations of sinful lifestyle, Paul continued his kind appellation in his second epistle. After scolding them in the first epistle, he again addressed them as saints: "To the church of God which is at Corinth, with all the saints who are in all Achaia; Grace to you and peace from God our Father and the Lord Jesus Christ" (2 Cor. 1:1–2).

The great apostle seemed to find saints everywhere. Writing from prison in Rome, he sent a letter to the believers in Philippi, the city founded in honor of King Philip, father of Alexander the Great. In the opening of his letter, he addressed it "to all the saints in Christ Jesus who are in Philippi, with the bishops and deacons" (Phil. 1:1). Following that same pattern, he wrote still another letter "to the saints and faithful brethren in Christ who are in Colosse" (Col. 1:2). These are just the times we see this designation on the pages of Paul's missionary letters, which were often circulated among the various churches. How many times he might have used this same designation in his personal encounters none of us will ever know. But if he so confidently could put such addresses in his public correspondence, it is highly probable that he sprinkled his daily dialogue with similar addresses. When Phoebe, Priscilla, Aquila, Andronicus, Urbanus, and others came to visit him in his Roman prison house (see Rom. 16 for a list of his many visitors) or on his travels to the various churches, he probably addressed them all as saints.

What Paul understood with unmistakable clarity was that no earthly church or pope ever makes anyone a saint. That is beyond the scope of anyone's ability or right. No matter how many times that foolish error may have occurred, a thousand or ten thousand repetitions of the error will not give it legitimacy. Furthermore, no one, no matter how godly and spiritual he might have been over decades of time, can ever earn or merit sainthood. If Mother Teresa had lived to be two hundred years old, her good deeds could not have guaranteed her one step inside heaven's doors. Paul's declarations in and by themselves could not merit sainthood for any person within his purview. Only the sacrificial atonement of Jesus Christ can make anyone a saint. That was the basis for Paul's addresses. He knew that Jesus Christ, the One whose life he had earlier despised, "chose us in Him before the foundation of the world, that we should be holy and without blame before Him in love" (Eph. 1:4). "In Him we have redemption through His blood, the forgiveness of sins, according to the riches of His grace" (v. 7). Through the act of justification, Christ has taken away all the sins, the guilt, and the filth of those who put their hope in Him. He is the one who makes us and designates us as saints, not the church, not the pope, and not the body of cardinals. Paul, serving as Christ's ambassador, speaks on behalf of his Lord and Master, who has every right to declare as saint anyone He wishes.

As a child of God, acting as His ambassador, His mouthpiece, do I have the right to address my children as Saint Richard, Saint Samantha, Saint Elijah, or Saint Gracie? Do I have the right to address my students as Saint Nathan, Saint Nicholas, Saint Jenna, or Saint Holly when they arrive at school some blustery morning?

The answer, I think, is a resounding but still cautious *yes!* Cautious, I say, because not everyone is entitled to such high honor or privilege, even if that person has been reared in a Christian home by godly parents. However, if that person has been born again and has been justified by the blood of the Savior, the title is appropriate. A second caution is that the believer has been led to understand that "by grace you have been saved through faith, and that not of yourselves; it is the gift of God, not of works, lest anyone should boast" (Eph. 2:8–9). Obviously such a designation could become an excuse for boasting, but that should never happen. Instead, the privilege of being called a saint ought make one blush with gratitude and humility. How can I be declared righteous in the eyes of an omniscient God, when He sees all the sins I still commit? How should I respond when He has taken all my guilt away and washed me clean as clean can be? Does the following plea apply to me?

> "Come now, and let us reason together,"
> Says the LORD,
> "Though your sins are like scarlet,
> They shall be as white as snow." (Isa. 1:18)

Some rebellious teenagers may bristle and sneer at such a designation, especially if it is applied by a teacher whom they prefer to hate, but being called saint may also give pause for serious reflection. Knowing that God has already forgiven the sins that they have recently committed may promote peace with their parents and teachers with whom they have been fighting. Maybe the rules of parents and teachers are tolerable after all! The wonderful reminder of unmerited favor may be the trigger that releases the pent-up frustrations associated with being a teenager in a confusing and vile world. Knowing that the guilt under which they daily stagger can all be lifted off their shoulders is sufficient ground on which to start afresh. It is worth the reminder!

6 What Must I Become?

In 1932 George Counts authored a book with the title *Dare the School Build a New Social Order?* That may seem like a dull, pedantic tome, well deserving of collecting dust on some musty library shelf. Ignore it and it will soon go away, one might expect.

But such did not happen. Even though the book has gone out of print, the title and the question keep resurfacing wherever thoughtful educators gather. Counts was not a lone wolf baying in the wilderness but a part of a vast movement that was deeply critical of society in general and communities in particular. He, along with his counterparts in the progressive education movement, was religiously upset about the rampant evils in the Western world during the 1920s and 1930s. They hoped to bring about certain social improvements through the influence of the schools.

Reflectors or Reformers?

Invited to watch a middle school football game in which my grandson was playing, I was appalled at the clothes that the seventh- and eighth-grade girls were wearing. Obviously wanting to accentuate their developing figures, they squeezed themselves into the tightest pants and blouses they could find. Then, with stunning success, they paraded past boys who were dressed in the baggiest pants imaginable. After a sufficient number of passes, they all muddled around each other in teenage frenzy. The football game was little more than a mercifully short battering of bodies into the dirt of the field, with nary a point being scored by either side. When the game finally ended at

7:00 P.M. I expected that all these juveniles would be picked up by parents and head for home and supper. But the opposite happened. As the game was winding down, a steady stream of cars brought even more students, who began milling, yelling, and screaming outside the gymnasium doors. Finally, at around 7:15, the doors swung open to the blasts of rock music. The school, so desirous of pleasing their teenage charges and placating their parents, had organized a midweek dance, complete with erotic music and gyrating activities.

Is there any wonder that junior high students regularly engage in fornication? Is it any wonder that middle school health departments pass out birth control devices to both sexes? Is it any wonder that Planned Parenthood clinics find plenty of clients wanting abortions for their teenage daughters? Is it any wonder that public schools across the land have failed miserably in the area of moral education?

The question that every educator has to ask is whether it is morally defensible to arrange such activities because the children and many of their parents want them. Would it not be better if the administrators and teachers refused to allow such sexually stimulating dances and rock concerts, insisting instead that the parents tend to their children's real needs at home? To even broach such policy matters is beyond the courage level of many public school employees. To deny their charges these seemingly harmless pleasures would invite threats of dismissal. Perish the thought if you want to preserve your position.

No matter how explosive and complicated the question may eventually become, it needs to be discussed in all seriousness if we are to do justice to the whole matter of moral education. We cannot judge a school as though it were an island in a sea of nothingness. The school, like the hand, is part of a larger body. The school does not exist in the middle of uninhabited deserts. It exists as part of a community, tied inextricably to that community in a variety of ways. It serves the parents who are and always will be, for good or for evil, the children's most influential teachers.

In trying to determine whether a particular school is a reflection of a community or a reforming agent trying to bring about change, we need to recognize that neither the school nor the community is a monolith or one-dimensional entity. That should be obvious, unless either is exceptionally small. Communities with any significant demographic diversity will have some persons who are superior in influence and power. They are the trendsetters and the controllers. Others, who may make up the unrecognizable majority, will probably give quiet assent and follow blindly along. The same is true within the school. In a normal and healthy situation it will be the principal or headmaster who determines the direction and controls the tempo. Those leaders, either within the school or within the community, are the ones to whom we need to look if we are to determine whether the answer comes up negative or affirmative.

The prime question, however, is not whether a school reflects the society it serves. Of course there is reflection. That is inevitable. The real question is whether a school should or ought to be a mirror. Can a quality school be merely a reflection?

One of the places to find out what a community's value are is in the high school parking lot. The number and types of cars parked there, either by teachers or by students, will disclose some clues as to what is and is not important. Teenagers are especially susceptible to putting their priorities on things that moth and rust quickly corrupt. Suppose the teaching staff, either in concert or individually, became critical of those values and set out to change them. Suppose some teacher, as a colleague of mine once did, went so far as to organize a field trip to the nearest junkyard and followed that with a lesson on the economics of the automobile. How many students and how many parents would sing that teacher's praises? Is it possible that the Son of God would say, "Well done, thou good and faithful teacher," even while the students pelted his house with excess tomatoes?

Suppose a second grader displays a measure of racial prejudice, well ingrained at home, and refers to black children by the *n* word. Suppose too that that very denigrating term is widely used by the non-black community. Should the teacher, upon hearing it, stop whatever she is doing and try to prevent that from happening again? If that community were Johannesburg, south Boston, or Detroit's east side, would that teacher have much chance of receiving a well-intentioned Christmas gift?

In a wide variety of ways kids echo the values and beliefs of their homes. Parents who live in academically oriented circles and who fill their homes with books, magazines, and newspapers are apt to have children who read not only at an early age but with above-average proficiency. Tightly knit college towns with a high percentage of college-educated residents are likely to have elementary and secondary schools where above-average achievement test scores are reported year after year. Can such towns boast an excellent school system, or should the board of directors honestly install a large looking glass in the entry?

A number of nonpublic elementary and secondary schools, some of them wearing the name "Christian," have resorted to the dubious procedures of setting their admission standards at arbitrarily high levels and then dismissing those who do not perform to satisfaction. When such practices are followed, it is predictable that the achievement levels will be high and that a large percentage of graduates will go on to postsecondary colleges. But by the standards of Scripture, such schools are not good; they are merely elitist.

Those who teach day after day can point to a myriad of other ways in which the students reflect or refract their parents. Athletically inclined parents, when allowed to vent their preferences, will make certain that physical education and athletic competition receive a disproportionate share of the curricular pie. The school had a good year, in their minds, if at least one of their teams made it to the state tournament. The parents who are musically or artistically inclined or prone to foreign travel will demonstrate their preferences for the curriculum, insisting on sizable allotments to the music, art, and foreign language programs. Even if their children choose not to enter their parents' professions, those students will likely be the ones who excel in those fields. There will be exceptions, for not every student wishes to please his or her parents.

During the late 1960s and early 1970s a number of young teachers incurred the wrath of many parents for both overt and covert suggestions that students break with their traditions and support the anti–Vietnam War movement. A large number of opportunistic teachers also seized upon the mood to promote their pet philosophies and to steer children away from beliefs that their parents long held dear. Questions of patriotism and religious conviction were raised to intense levels throughout the world. In Canada, England, Germany, and Japan, as well as the United States, thousands and even millions of young people were being taught that it was wrong to reflect their parents' positions. Naturally, fathers and mothers reacted with righteous indignation.

When this explosive situation occurred, many parents assumed that the schools were going to the dogs and that they could never be good again until the upstart, hippie faculty were purged from the system. They were probably right in many cases. But such educational turmoil has happened many times before and will continue to occur until the Savior comes again.

Around four hundred years before Jesus was born there was a school in Athens in which the head teacher questioned the democratic values and behavior of the beloved polis. The community reaction and the harassment from officials were so strong that the teacher finally drank hemlock and died. That person, of course, was Socrates, whom most of the world venerates until this day. Approximately fifteen hundred years later there was a German monk whose responsibility it was to oversee the instruction in eleven Augustinian monasteries. A district superintendent of parochial education, we would call him. When he began to read the Bible seriously, he also began to teach some ideas that broke sharply with tradition. Trying to reform the schools from within, Martin Luther was not only rebuked but driven into hiding because there was a price on his head.

During the period following the Civil War thousands of capable and dedicated teachers labored in the Freedmen's Schools of the American South. Their driving passion was to teach illiterate adults and anxious children the skills and rewards of reading, as well as civic responsibility. Because of the color of those students, the teachers were driven out of town, often wearing a coat of tar and feathers.

Just before and after World War I there were numerous other incidents for which we as Christians need to be ashamed. Because of the impending war with Germany and Austria, many superpatriots in the United States decreed that it was wrong for schools and churches to teach, sing, or play German music. When that long list of sacred and classical composers of Deutsch descent is reviewed, it becomes apparent that some of the best music was outlawed. Could schools be considered quality institutions for making and enforcing such objectionable rules? To most of us, the doubts are real. Yet the teachers and administrators who complied with such community wishes were considered the good old boys.

The most obvious example of all, one that should not require a great deal of elaboration, is that of Christ. Although many Christians refuse to think of Christ as a teacher and many non-Christians see Him as nothing more than a pedagogue, we can learn much from the account of His experiences. During the first part of His public teaching ministry, crowds of students listened to Him intently and followed Him wherever He went. As long as they misunderstood the Master, they worshiped Him and wanted to hear His lessons. Once they began to understand His message, however, they did everything to silence Him and finally crucified Him on a shameful cross. He came preaching repentance, but they wanted nothing of that.

The Need for Change

Anyone who understands the nature of the educational process will recognize that change within the educand is at the heart of learning. Scripture expresses the demand clearly when it calls us to be transformed by the daily renewing of our minds. Our attitudes, beliefs, values, and skills must continuously undergo change and adjustment if we are to become the kinds of people we ought to be.

Change is often necessary. No school anywhere on this earth can consider itself to be perfect. There is always room for improvement. Significant alteration, however, never comes without a struggle, for change is always accompanied by resistance. None of us easily or happily succumbs to reformation in our lives, unless it is a sudden influx of money that allows us to purchase some long-desired goods. Schools, like individuals, may be overjoyed with new-found prosperity, but even in such situations someone has to pay the piper, suggesting a less than ecstatic change in someone's payment pattern.

Our purpose is not to chronicle every change that might occur in any given year. To do such would be unprofitable, for we might merely be reflecting the changes occurring in the community, with the school being nothing more than a reflection. Our basic question would then still be unanswered, for we need to know if the school should attempt to transform the society it serves.

In the context of Christian education the answer ought to be relatively clear. Christian teachers, working in concert with Christian parents and Christian pastors, are always seeking the daily transformation of students' lives by the daily renewing of their minds. It is not a matter of parents against teachers or administrators versus the board of directors. When an adversarial situation develops, as too often happens, there is a breakdown either in communications or among human relationships. Such is not ideal and not indicative of excellence in operation. Yet breakdowns do occur as persons attempt to walk the uphill road of sanctification.

The truly good school system will resolve such difficulties according to the dictates of Scripture. Parents and teachers, seeing each other as co-workers within the body of Christ, will respond to each other as Christians and not as antagonists. Instead of seeking their own selfish ends, each will be concerned primarily with the other's welfare. Instead of peddling rumors and hurling insults, each will speak the truth in love, directly to the person with whom the disagreement has occurred. Instead of pitting student against teacher or pupil against parent, all the involved parties will bow before God and His Word, seeking His direction for their lives.

These formulas won't always be effective. No one ever said that living the Christian life is going to be easy. Christ never promised His followers a flowery bed of ease. He did, however, detail a mode of operation that must be followed if His teachers, His parents, and His children are to receive that commendation, "Well done, thou good and faithful servant."

The Confrontational Classroom

One of my colleagues used to end every morning coffee break with the pronouncement, "Well, people, it is time to go to clash." Occasionally someone would challenge his abuse of the English language, but never sufficiently to make him change his habits. Off to "clash" he would march, textbooks and notes in hand. Lou wasn't an ornery, contentious sort of guy, and he didn't have the reputation of being mean or disputatious. But he did have a reputation of being somewhat liberal in his viewpoints and was known to present his defenses of his positions with animated vigor.

Was Lou onto something? Did he know something about the nature of formal instruction that I should also grasp? Or did he merely get his daily jollies by mispronouncing a word? Since I also had a reputation of loving to stir up lively discussion in the classroom, I developed a liking for his deadpan humor about "going off to clash." What fun to shake these young folks, who were so enamored with the opposite sex, with sports, with television's daily mush of soap operas, to the core of their cultural infatuation. What fun to cause them sleepless nights by assigning them to define a simple word like education, only to watch them cough out indefensible kinds of definitions. What delight in forcing them to confront the illogical, unscientific, and even preposterous theory of evolution, to defend it with hard logic, with facts rather than with opinions, and with biblical proof. After all, if God really used evolution as His means of bringing the world into existence, would it not be expected that this same God would have talked about that subject in pages of His written revelation? Would it be unreasonable to ask these students or some of my colleagues to prove theistic evolution from the pages of Holy Writ?

What pained expressions crept across students' faces when they were asked to explain such commonplace terms as freedom or to defend the proposition that all truth is relative. What agony when they had to explain the relationship between the kingdom of God and democracy, when their catechism told them that "Thy kingdom come" is a prayer for all men everywhere to give up their claims to autonomy and to turn their lives over in total submission to the King of the universe. How could that be, when America's greatest national leaders had preached democracy, with its overarching claim that the people rule and that all law originates with man? How can the kingdom of God be palatable if two world wars have been fought to make the world safe for democracy?

Lou might have been on target when it came to advanced college courses, but could he also have spoken wisely enough to encompass secondary and elementary classrooms? Would it be feasible or defensible to challenge thirteen- or sixteen-year-old students in junior and senior high with such intellectual confrontation? Should they not be fed a diet of simple facts and then be asked to regurgitate them on Friday's test? Were not repetition and memorization the real stuff of education? Was not repetition the mother of all learning, as the Jesuits insisted? Was there something inherent in the educational process that required confrontation? Was conflict at the essence of education? Should every teacher, at every level, be "going off to clash"?

During the decades of the 1970s and the 1980s B. F. Skinner ruled the world of educational psychology and foisted on classrooms the world over his erratic notion of behavior modification. On initial contact, the term almost sounds biblical. Isn't that what Paul was talking about in Romans 12:1–2 and Colossians 3, and what Peter pushed passionately in the fourth chapter of his first epistle? Had not these biblical writers argued persistently that we have to "put off the old man of sin and put on the new man in Christ"? Paul had concluded so pointedly that the application of the gospel message is that you and I have to be transformed by the daily renewing of our minds. Because all of us are sinners and because our behavior is contrary to the law of God, all of us must have our wicked behavior modified.

But that is not what Skinner or any of his disciples meant. Evolutionists to the core, they so twisted their own minds and theories that even the devil must have shaken his head at some of their writings. *Beyond Freedom and Dignity* was an overt attempt to replace freedom with manipulative mind control and, simultaneously, to demand that behavior be changed without ever saying that any behavior was wrong. How stupid, how impossible, and yet how tremendously popular. When wrong answers were discovered on a spelling test, in a history quiz, or in an English grammar exercise, it was, according to these theoreticians, impermissible to mark those answers as wrong. To put a check mark alongside a misspelled word or to use a red pen to identify errors on the English test was not to be tolerated. Every good teacher, they argued, was to reward the right answers and to ignore the wrong ones. They could never deny that there were wrong answers, but they blindly concluded that you might not tell that to the student. The only right way to control behavior was to reward, preferably with M&Ms, the correct answers.

Such teaching strategies would help students' brains to become filled with the desirable data.

Skinner was so obsessed with John Locke's theory of the tabula rasa that he reared his daughter in a glass box so as to control and keep out any undesirable stimuli. Convinced that the child was blank at birth and void of any evil, he placed his infant daughter inside an air crib that had controlled temperature and atmosphere so that he could monitor the total range of influences on her life. The experiment was a colossal failure, for he soon began to realize the cruel nonsense of trying to confine a two- or three-year-old child in a glass box no bigger than a dog's pen. Her later life, not surprisingly, was hardly a model of either freedom or dignity.

Blindly, though, the world of educational planners and school administrators followed Skinner, convinced that original sin and total depravity were bogeymen of the Reformation and not worthy of belief by the academic community. Forced to admit by events all around them that there was a propensity for evil in this world, they ascribed it to the environment and never to the inherent character of man.

But how should the teacher confront Samantha or Nathan or any other child who makes a mistake in the classroom? For the child's own sanity, he or she needs to know whether the answers were right or wrong. Not telling a person that his answer is wrong, when he knows that it obviously is, is cruelty of the highest sort. Students cannot stand a teacher who doesn't know the difference between right and wrong or cannot choose one theory over another but vacillates like a feather in the wind. Samantha is not fooled when her teacher says, "Isn't it wonderful that you had eleven good answers? You will get your reward at the end of the day!" She is not so stupid as to forget about the other nine answers, with which she struggled and at which she finally guessed. Why won't the teacher tell me that they are wrong? Why won't the teacher sit down with me and tell me the truth?

But the confrontational character of the classroom takes on another hue when we consider not only the acquisition of information, or the development of academic skills, but also the confrontation with behavior. If Samantha, Nathan, Craig, and Holly were little angels, incapable of any evil behavior, there would be nothing to confront.

But if they and every other elementary child are inclined by nature to hate both God and his neighbor, we can expect some hair pulling, some deliberate defiance to the teacher's commands, some mean-spirited teasing, and some subtle lying. What is a teacher to do when she observes Nathan pulling Holly's hair or Susan looking at a crib sheet during Friday's spelling test? What is she to do when Nick trips Ian as he walks down the classroom aisle? What is she to do when the children will not stop talking while she is trying to explain something? Must she wait for them to do something sweet and nice and then promise them a reward for being so good? Must she confront the classroom bully? Must she confront the cheater? Must she confront the whole class and demand that they show courteous respect to those placed in authority over them? Of course she must.

The question for many will be not whether but how. How can a teacher most effectively confront a class that will not stop talking after they have come in from recess break? How can a teacher deal with the lying and the cheating that goes on in every classroom? How should a teacher respond to the students who drive many teachers out of the profession?

First of all, the classroom teacher better be realistic enough to expect such behavior. The naive college graduate who has overdosed on Skinnerian or behaviorist psychology will enter the classroom with an awful handicap. The one who has rejected the doctrines of original sin and total depravity will be so naive and misguided that his tenure as a teacher will be brief. The first requirement of any good teacher is that she knows the students whom she is trying to teach. That implies that she knows them truly and not falsely. Having a vision of what you want them to become always implies a clear vision of what they currently are. The *ought* is always preceded by the *is*. To think of children as blank slates or as empty buckets waiting and wanting to be filled is naiveté of the most flagrant sort. To think of them as coming into the world with no inherent values or knowledge or sense of right is to adopt the image of John Dewey, who saw children as nothing more than cultural products, the accumulated sum of environmental influences.

To adopt such an attitude is to conclude that the environment causes all deviant behavior and that all deviant persons are victims who bear no responsibility for their actions. The teenage alcoholic is addicted to strong drink because of his friends and the home in which he was reared. The young girl who assaults her teacher acts that way because she has watched too much television and too many R-rated movies. The inner-city kids who refuse to do their math assignments and who cannot read by sixth grade are victims of the inner-city culture. The white rednecks who mutter the *n* word and then drive black students off the playground have been overly influenced by the white supremacist movements. The environment must be changed, not the person. The environment is the culprit, while the victim is to be coddled and pitied.

Then, when things go haywire, the first order of business is to trek to the state assemblyman's office and demand more money for the public's schools. If that doesn't work, then search out a lawyer who will sue someone or some organization who may have had control over that environment. The prerequisite is that someone be endowed with deep enough pockets to pay the lawyer and to give the plaintiff easy access to easy street. To confront the individual student who is disrespectful, lazy, naughty, disobedient, and in search of sexual gratification or drugs is too risky. He may take his dad's loaded revolver along in his backpack and blow your brains out.

Confrontation is risky business. In many classrooms and schools, there is little or nothing to fear, for parents intuitively know that their cherubs are capable of crimes. But, in growing numbers of others, the risk is growing by leaps and bounds. That is nothing new, for man has always been in need of transformation. That was the message of Moses, who confronted the idolatrous Israelites for building a golden calf to assist their worship. That was the message of the prophet Nathan, who came to King David after he had committed adultery with Bathsheba and had arranged to have her husband, Uriah, killed. That was the message of Isaiah, who was commissioned by God to be His ambassador to Israel at the height of her sinful state, coming as a divinely appointed prosecutor who brought charges and accusations of evil against this disobedient people (Isa. 1). That was also the assignment of Jeremiah, a hundred years later, who had to proclaim the impending arrival of exile and destruction for unrepented sins (Jer. 1). These prophets, like any teacher today, were not embraced and loved for confronting wrong behavior and sinful attitudes. On the contrary, both Isaiah and Jeremiah had to fear for their lives, and Jeremiah was thrown into a slime hole for confronting the religious leaders of his day (Jer. 38:1–13).

Confronting the religious leaders of His day was the frequent mark of Jesus Christ. Coming as "the Messenger of the covenant" (Mal. 3:1), Jesus went to the seat of power and authority and there confronted the high priests, the scribes, the Pharisees, and the Sadducees with a powerful accusation that made their blood boil in response. Even His disciples had to be confronted on numerous occasions, as when Peter insisted that his master not go to Jerusalem. When the master Teacher confronted Peter, He rebuked his tempestuous disciple with a stern reminder that Peter was acting more like the devil than like his Lord (Matt. 16:23). True to Malachi's prophecy, Jesus headed directly to the temple court when He entered Jerusalem, upbraiding the ungodly with stinging rebuke and well-placed condemnation. Christ was not only confrontational; He was also a "controversialist," to borrow a term from John R. Stott's classic book.[1] Jesus dared to confront all those who committed sin, calling them to repentance and reaping the anger of those he offended.

One need not stop there, for the apostle Paul seemed to search out opportunities for confrontation. Before his conversion on the Damascus road, he searched out those hated followers of the Way, for he was convinced that they were wrong and needed to be corrected, forcibly if more gentle persuasion were not effective. After his conversion he did not change his pattern, even though he did change the object of his searches. Now he went first to the synagogues, where the Jewish people needed to change their mind about the "blasphemer" that they had so disgracefully hung on a cross as a public spectacle. Whenever those Jews demonstrated with unmistakable certainty that they would not change their minds, he then went to search out Gentiles, even going into the bastion of Hellenistic philosophy and confronting the leading thinkers of Greece.

Confrontation also caused the apostle many unpleasant consequences, which he recites in his letter to the Corinthian church. For all of his efforts, he was rewarded five times with whippings. Three times he was beaten with rods, once he was stoned and left for dead, three times he was shipwrecked, and often he was imprisoned for his preaching (2 Cor. 11:24–27). None of those violent experiences could stop him, for Paul knew with the greatest clarity that all of us must be transformed if we are to become compliant with the gospel.

The tragedy of American culture, which has come to expression so powerfully in Littleton, is that for years and years parents, teachers, administrators, boards, or counselors did not dare to confront deviant behavior. They didn't dare to cross their psychology professors, whom they silently worshiped. They didn't dare to confront their own kids and tell them, in clear, unmistakable terms, that their behavior was unacceptable and would not be tolerated. Collectively, they acted like the foolish old prophet Eli, who did not challenge the wicked actions of his sons Hophni and Phinehas (1 Sam. 2:12, 22–24; 4:11) and finally had to experience a slaughter of people as a consequence for their neglect. To not confront evil when it pokes its ugly head in your face is evil of the worst sort.

——7 What Must the Child Learn?

For two years my wife and I found it necessary to place our children in a public school. Though all our family experiences had centered in Christian schools, circumstances placed us in a community where there was no Christian school. This new experience was good for all of us, not because the education was excellent but because we had opportunity to learn firsthand something of the character of public schools in America. My work as an educator had brought me into many public schools for short periods of time, but never on a sustained basis and never from the vantage point of a parent.

Despite the legal restrictions and the presumed wall of separation between religion and education, our two younger children had fine Christian teachers whose values and perspective we could often share. Our eldest son was in junior high and had a quite different set of circumstances. One of his teachers was the most rabid evolutionist we had ever encountered. Another was a rock music fanatic who specialized in the offbeat. Other faculty members represented middle-class, secular American values. The principal saw his role as the great pacifier, trying to please everyone so that each person could exercise his libertarian options and have his own way.

In such situations the child, and especially the adolescent, can easily be pulled mentally asunder and lose direction or purpose for life. The majority of students in that school gave the impression that they were confused kids who didn't know what they believed or where they were going. Like blind sheep, they passionately followed the person who sounded most convincing and sincere at the time. Recent teaching opportunities in public high schools have convinced me that not much has changed.

Robert Ulich, a noted educational analyst, recently condemned American schools when he wrote,

> Looking back at education as it has been during the past decades and as it is still today in many places, one discovers a frantic emphasis on science, but at the same time a frightening lack of truly human purpose. Apparently education has alienated itself from the perennial concerns of mankind.[1]

One does not have to look far in America's public schools to find the scenes about which Ulich was writing. The same conditions often are true for Christian schools as well, for they sometimes lose their way and run off in a multitude of directions at once. Far too often, the lament is heard that people do not know why Christian schools exist or what they are trying to accomplish.[2] In formal schooling there seems to be a great deal of confusion and aimless wandering. Such should not deter or distract the Christian, however. The apostle Paul, in his letter to the Philippians, reminds us that we should be like the runner in a race who looks straight ahead and keeps his eyes fixed on the goal that is set before him (Phil. 3:13–14; cf. 2 Tim. 4:7; Heb. 12:1). Remembering that principle, we should not turn to the public schools to see what they are doing, but we should focus our eyes in God's Holy Word to see what kind of goal or what sets of objectives He has spelled out for us. After all, the children temporarily entrusted to our care are His possession (1 Cor. 6:19–20).

Merely knowing that the Bible contains the answers we seek does not automatically guarantee that we will find those answers. Like the vast majority of educators, we do not know how to proceed or what precisely it is for which we should look. If we state the problem or phrase the question badly, we may look for years and never find the answers. For example, we could ask the question in any of the following forms:

1. *What is our school's educational objective?* Phrased this way, we might turn for our answer to Proverbs 22:6: "Train up a child in the

way he should go, and when he is old he will not depart from it." That text has been a guiding light for Christian educators for decades and even centuries, but it is hardly exhaustive in meaning and fails to shed light on such legitimate questions as to whether we should study modern math or traditional arithmetic. It would be easy if God had set aside one chapter or book in which He clearly spelled out all educational objectives for the twenty-first century, but He has seen fit not to fragment the gospel in that way.

2. *What are you trying to accomplish?* Such a phrasing of the question legitimately focuses on educational goals, but it assumes that the source of answers lies with the teacher. Such a question compels introspection and self-examination, worthwhile activities in themselves, but it hardly elicits answers that can transcend individual human weakness.

3. *What should our teachers teach?* At the high school and college levels, this is the most common form of question used to unravel the riddle of educational objectives. Because it is so common, it is necessary to call special attention to how it is answered.

When confronted with the third question, most teachers beyond the elementary level respond by saying that they should teach the subjects in which they majored or specialized at college or grad school. In spite of their enthusiasm, it is philosophically ridiculous to say that we should teach math or history or biology or music. It would make as much sense for a farmer to say that he was trying to raise corn planters or produce tractors. It would make as much sense to say that carpenters are trying to build hammers, saws, and nails.

Obviously these statements do not make much sense, yet many of our supposedly best educators are often confused to the point where they do not know what they are talking about. They have become so subject-centered that they have lost clarity of vision and long-range perspective.

Why do we not say that a farmer should produce tractors? Or a carpenter build hammers? Or a teacher teach history? Because the tractor and the hammer and the history are tools with which to produce something else. They are the means, the implements, and not the ends or objectives. Those people have failed to grasp the distinction between ends and means. The curricular subjects are the tools of the teacher's profession.

Countless teachers have the uncanny knack for avoiding the question of purpose and turn instead to questions of means or methodology. If a carpenter spent his best energy analyzing his tools and never set his sights on the cabinet or house to be constructed, we would soon dismiss him from the job. When teachers do that, however, we honor them with a promotion and call them professor.

What Learning Is Most Valuable?

If we are to find the answers to the questions of purpose, we need to avoid the pitfalls of badly phrased questions. We need to turn our attention, for the moment, away from the subjects of curriculum and teachers. That is not to say that curriculum and teachers are unimportant. Nothing could be further from the truth, but turning our attention in another direction is necessary if we are to avoid the fallacies of both the subject-centered and the teacher-centered schools.

The proper focus for determining correct and clear objectives is the child or student who must acquire learning. We need to ask, What must the child learn? We need to be reminded that children are creatures of God, made in His image. We need also to remember that the redeemed of the Lord have been bought by the blood of Jesus Christ and therefore belong to Him in a special relationship. We need then to ask what He wants them to learn. We need also to be reminded that we all need to be transformed from what is to what ought to be, from what we are to what we should become.

This required transformation becomes most apparent when we observe and analyze our youth. In table 3, note the obvious changes that are clearly implied if a child is to progress from being to becoming.

Table 3. Learning Objectives

BEING ➤	BECOMING	NEEDS TO LEARN
nonreader	reader	to read
poor speller	good speller	to spell words correctly
scribbler	good writer	to write legibly
computer klutz	computer whiz	to master the computer
immature	mature	to handle responsibility
awkward	coordinated	to control muscles
monotone	a good singer	to read musical scales
ignorant	knowledgeable	to know the truth
gullible	wise	to discern between true and false
scared	confident	to overcome fear

Learning and teaching, when so perceived, are essentially aimed at and explanatory of changes that need to occur in the learner. Such an approach, in contrast to those suggested in preceding paragraphs, helps us to see objectives most clearly, for it focuses directly on the learning to be acquired and not on the persons or means responsible for producing that learning. But here too is a potential pitfall, for it would be easy to slip into the errors of child-centeredness or to embrace the philosophy of John Dewey.

Consider the question: Is "value" a verb or a noun? When you consider the use and meaning of this word, should you begin by using it as a verb? Is value something first of all that you and I do? Or should we assume that value exists before we do anything? Do things have value before you and I begin to value them?

Watch how you answer that, for the way you respond will link you either to Christians or to atheistic evolutionists. Dewey posed the question, insisting that nothing has any value until you and I place value on it. Valuing is a strictly human activity, which we begin to exercise by our priorities and by assigning worth to sundry kinds of choices. As an atheistic evolutionist, Dewey denied the presence and power of God and insisted that all socializing and valuing activity begins with man. Just as man is a product of his culture, so the values that are placed on things are a result of human effort. Value for Dewey was always a verb before it became a noun.

Much American culture in recent decades has not put a value on babies that are still in the womb. Therefore there is no harm done by abortion because those "blobs of tissue" have no value until they have left the birth canal and are held in their mother's arms. Then suddenly they become worth keeping. In the Netherlands or in some segments of American society, old people have no value, so there is no harm in practicing euthanasia. It is merciful to put old, sick folks out of their existence. So go the terribly wrong-headed arguments.

You and I have to ask another question, though. Does God have a system of values? Are some things more important than others to the God who has made us? Has God placed comparative values on different parts of His creation? Does God value humans more highly than crickets? Does He value an obedient heart more than ritualistic practice? Are there values on things before humans ever begin to value them? Are there eternal values that you and I must try to understand and to imitate?

When questions about educational objectives or goals are seriously asked, it soon becomes apparent that there are hundreds and even thousands of legitimate answers. When that happens, it becomes necessary to divert attention to the matter of taxonomy or categories of answers. If, for example, even fifty or a hundred answers were given, some grouping would have to occur. The most common taxonomy used today is that advanced by the secularist Benjamin Bloom and found in most secular textbooks. In its essential form, the categories or groupings are cognitive, affective, and psychomotor. The cognitive is best translated as intellectual or academic, the affective as personal or emotional, and the psychomotor as physical.

This taxonomy is uncritically accepted by millions of schoolmen and has often been refined in attempts to delineate minute concerns, but it fails miserably when confronted with basic and simple problems. For example, would learning to sing be classified as intellectual, personal, or physical? Obviously the body is involved in such learning activity, for one could not sing without exercising the vocal chords, the diaphragm, the mouth, the lungs, the ears, and many lesser parts. So too the affective area, for singing is clearly an emotional or personal expression, conveying attitudes and feelings on every score. Not to slight the musician, we must also recognize that the mind or intellect is involved. Not all academes would quietly concur, but the point should require no further demonstration.

The same type of problem occurs if we try to fit such learning as typing, writing, or spelling into Bloom's taxonomy. In such a learning activity, and every other, the total person is involved, not just his fingers or his voice box or his brain. The whole organic person learns, with every part of his person involved in every learning occasion. To argue otherwise is both to fragment the person into disjointed parts and to reduce a total learning experience to its most visible component.

In an attempt to separate itself from the contemporary secular mindset, Christian Schools International (CSI) some years ago commissioned its resident educational philosopher to draft a new taxonomy for learning goals. The finished and accepted product bore a fresh configuration, composed of intellectual, moral-decisional, and creative categories. The external break with secular thought was obvious, but the internal weaknesses were identical. By testing this taxonomy against such legitimate goals as learning to sing, to read, to type, to pray, or to write, one finds again that the objectives encompass all three categories, with none claiming exclusive right. Again, this taxonomy, devised for CSI by Henry Beversluis, does violence to the wholeness of man and attempts to divorce the singing voice not only from the imagination but also from the obedient heart and the ever operative mind. Given a simple choice, one would be hard-pressed to choose the category for any of the preceding goals.

The key to effective categorizing or taxonomy lies not in disjointing the learner but in seeing clearly the relationship between taxonomy and axiology, which is the study of values. Educational objectives must be categorized, for large, unruly numbers of objectives can be identified as legitimate. What must be emphasized is that not all objectives are equally important or valuable. Since everyone has some kind of value system, it becomes apparent that not all will be of equal value. Some will be of great value, while others must be of lesser or minimal value.

Rate the following educational objectives, on a scale of 1 to 4, according to their importance (1 = the highest value or primary, and 4 = the least value or incidental). There is no specific distribution of numbers.

Children need to learn
_____ to use a computer
_____ to count to ten
_____ to obey their fathers
_____ to ride a bicycle
_____ to dissect a frog
_____ to write in cursive
_____ to share assets generously
_____ to drive a car
_____ to trust and obey God
_____ to forgive others
_____ to write clearly and well
_____ important historical dates
_____ to appreciate beauty
_____ to respect their teachers
_____ to love their neighbors
_____ to pray to God
_____ to speak a foreign language
_____ to roller skate
_____ to read the Bible
_____ to discern between truth and falsehood
_____ to identify types of leaves
_____ to do three-column addition
_____ to love their siblings
_____ to play the piano
_____ to accept defeat gracefully
_____ to spell correctly
_____ to control their temper
_____ important Bible truths
_____ to tell time
_____ to be totally honest
_____ to dress themselves
_____ to make pipe bombs

This taxonomy avoids the pitfalls of both the Bloom and the CSI systems, while allowing us to differentiate which ones we consider most important and which can be ignored or given little attention.

Over the years I have had numerous opportunities to use this exercise with many school groups. Some of them were parents' and grandparents' groups. Others were Christian school teachers. Many were teachers in training. Some were public school professionals. One thing became apparent whenever I ran the test. When I was dealing with a mixture of non-Christian people, the value ratings would be widely scattered. When I was dealing with people who were united in their Christian faith commitments, the answers were highly uniform. When I was dealing with a wide range of age groups, the answers would again become quite disparate. It is no secret, for example, that sixteen-year-old students have different values than do forty-year-old parents. It is also no secret that music teachers have different values than do physical education teachers.

What was most revealing were the types of responses that I got in public school settings as compared with those in Christian school or church settings. To catch some of that difference, go back over the list one more time. This time, cross out the objectives that either are not or may not be taught in the typical public school. After you have gone through the list, take note of any pattern that has developed. If you are a Christian, I suspect that you will find that you have crossed out primarily those which you have earlier marked with a 1, those which are of primary importance to you. The objectives that the Christian finds to be most valued are the very ones that have been outlawed or ignored in the public school setting. Therein lies the major difference between the two school systems.

Is that difference worth the monthly tuition bill? Is that difference sufficient ground for sending your child to the private or parochial school down the road? Is that difference enough reason to consider home schooling your children next year?

Which Learning Is Most Painful?

In the preceding section we focused on the matter of values, trying to determine which of the learning goals in the school are of the greatest value. Having worked our way through that exercise, we need to ask a further question: Which of those many learning goals involves the most pain and frustration? That may seem to be an unimportant or even illegitimate question. The skeptics among us might still be asking, "Is pain essential to the learning process? Isn't all proper learning sheer delight and joy? Are not the successful teachers the ones who make learning fun and whose classrooms are filled with smiling, happy faces? Isn't the presence of pain, anger, and frustration a sign of poor teaching?"

The answer, I want to insist, is that all learning involves, of necessity, some measure of pain. Not all learning involves the same amount of pain, just as all learning does not involve the same measure of difficulty. Some learning, my students have repeatedly reminded me, is inherently more difficult and more painful than is others. Some learning, I must also insist, is more rewarding—producing more joy and pleasure—than is others. Not everything in this life is of equal value and significance, for if everything measured exactly the same on a numerical scale, there would cease to be any need for discussing value, since all value would be the same.

The message was driven home again when my wife and I met some new friends from the Netherlands. We had some time on our hands, and so we offered to teach them a new game we had found exciting. It is fairly complex and is called "Heartland Strategy." We printed the rules, walked them through an entire game, and then asked them to play one round for real. They made a series of mistakes and repeated some a number of times, but they quickly found themselves enjoying the game immensely. Their learning curve was short and sharp. For two weeks we couldn't keep them away from the door.

At the same time, from another quarter, we and our Dutch friends were invited by some Egyptian pastors to learn a few elementary Arabic words and sentences. One doesn't have to look at written Arabic for long, or listen for long, to realize that learning to speak Arabic is far more complex than is a board game involving playing cards and pegs on a board. The reaction of our friends was a firm and almost impolite "No, thank you." They were still smarting too much from the pain and frustration of having to use broken English with us to attempt still another language. They resisted every teaching effort put forth by our Egyptian friends.

Take a minute or two to rate the following objectives, first (on the left side of the blank) by the amount of pain, frustration, or difficulty you associate with each objective. Indicate your response by using MP for "most pain," AP for "average pain," and LP for "least pain." Don't think in terms of physical pain so much as emotional difficulty or frustration. Consider, for example, the kind of anxiety associated with that learning and the length of time needed for mastery.

_____ / ____ Learning to use a computer
_____ / ____ Learning to count to ten
_____ / ____ Learning to obey your father
_____ / ____ Learning to ride a bicycle
_____ / ____ Learning to dissect a frog
_____ / ____ Learning to write in cursive
_____ / ____ Learning to share assets generously
_____ / ____ Learning to drive a car
_____ / ____ Learning to trust and obey God
_____ / ____ Learning to forgive others
_____ / ____ Learning to write clearly and well
_____ / ____ Learning important historical dates
_____ / ____ Learning a foreign language
_____ / ____ Learning to roller skate
_____ / ____ Learning to sing a tune
_____ / ____ Learning to discern between truth and falsehood
_____ / ____ Learning to identify types of leaves
_____ / ____ Learning to do three-column addition
_____ / ____ Learning to love my siblings
_____ / ____ Learning to play the piano
_____ / ____ Learning to accept defeat
_____ / ____ Learning to spell correctly
_____ / ____ Learning to control my temper
_____ / ____ Learning important biblical truths

After you complete this exercise, go over the list again. This time (on the right side of the blank), rate each of the objectives by the amount of joy or satisfaction associated with that learning. Those which gave you the most joy and sense of satisfaction, rate with an MJ, for "most joy." For those yielding "average joy," label with AJ. Finally, those producing the "least joy" or satisfaction, label with an LJ. When you have completed both exercises, look for correlations. Are the ones labeled as MP also the ones you labeled as MJ? Are those with the LP designation also the ones with the LJs? Is there a significant correlation between those with the highest value and those with the most significant pain and satisfaction? Are those learning experiences which are most important the ones that are most difficult but also the ones that produce the greatest sense of satisfaction and accomplishment?

Over thirty years of training and supervising teachers, a clear pattern developed. Whenever I asked students to perform these exercises, there was a very high correlation between significance or value and emotional intensity. Objectives considered to be of greatest value were also those which exacted the greatest emotional toll over the longest period of time. An objective such as learning to ride a bicycle, although producing initial fear of falling, was rather quickly mastered but soon lost its significance. Learning to love and obey one's parents, however, took much greater time to learn and involved long periods of frustration, but it also brought the greatest rewards when finally attained. In the same way, learning to play a musical instrument, while taking years to achieve mastery, did not measure up to the significance or frustration of learning to discern between truth and falsehood.

In my own lifetime, it took me twenty years to learn to respect, obey, and love my father, not because he was a tyrant or because I was such a rebel. In retrospect, my dad was often thought to favor me, which brought me no small amount of teasing from my siblings. Yet it took almost two decades for me to come to that point where I truly respected and loved him. Finally, after some intense challenges from both sides, I began to realize that Father knew best. From that point on, the pain of sour relationships was gone and I could enjoy a peace that passes all understanding. Numerous young people down through the decades have shared similar experiences, most often with their fathers but also with their mothers.

To Prove the Point

To suggest, even faintly, that the primary purpose of teaching is to produce some desired change or series of changes in the learner is to embark on a risky adventure. It is like walking on too-thin ice before the subzero temperatures have formed a foot-thick layer. It is like walking on eggs when the chickens are watching. It is somewhat akin to telling a rebellious teenager that his choice of music is unacceptable. The consequences are not apt to be pleasant.

If I were the only one making such a bold and bald assertion, I would do so with fear and trepidation. But I am not alone anymore, although there were many years when I thought that no one saw what seemed so clear to me. I was emboldened some years ago when CSI distributed a promotional bulletin boldly proclaiming "When God calls us through His Son, Jesus Christ, He changes us completely so that we become totally committed to serving and glorifying Him" (CSI bulletin cover, 1990).

The CSI staff had not always been so forward looking. For years, it seemed, they had been reluctant to equate learning with planned change. Since the late 1960s I had encouraged such an approach, but with very limited success. Along the road, Nicholas Wolterstorff had also pushed the agenda of change through his excellent book, *Educating for Responsible Action*. In the introduction he wrote,

> Those who teach do so with a variety of aims. For the purpose of our discussion in this book we shall be concentrating on only one of these: the aim of producing, or occasioning, desired *changes* in the persons being taught. . . . We shall consider only three. . . .
>
> One type of alteration a teacher will characteristically seek is an increase in the student's awareness of what is true. The *change* being sought is one from ignorance to knowl-

edge, or from a false belief—or no belief—about something to a true belief. We might call [such] . . . *cognitive* learning.

A second type of *change* promoted by a person who is teaching someone else may be an increase in ability or capability, competence or skill. This type of learning we might call *ability* learning.

Third, those who teach characteristically aim at altering the inclinations or dispositions of their students to act in certain ways in various types of situations. The increase or decrease of some inclination or disposition as the result of a learning or training process may be called *tendency* learning.[3]

One person who has seen most clearly the necessity of equating learning with change is Jay E. Adams, longtime seminary professor and the genius behind the National Association of Nouthetic Counselors. Committed to a biblically based approach to counseling, the association has relied heavily on books that Adams has written over the last few decades. At the heart of that approach is the realization that most psychological problems are caused by sin in the troubled person's life. Instead of seeing interpersonal conflict as the consequence of a bad environment, nouthetic counselors (sometimes preferring the title "biblical counselors") look first at the lifestyle of the person to determine if there are spiritual problems for which the person must repent. Sin requires admission of guilt and then genuine repentance in order for that person to avoid problems of despair and all its manifestations.

For example, if a marriage is falling apart, it is foolish to treat the problem as rooted in one's physiology if it is known that one partner has been unfaithful to the other. No amount of medication or therapy will overcome the sin and guilt that inevitably come with adultery. That marriage will not be healed if the changes are only outward. To that end Adams argues,

> Outward change may appear good to others, even to oneself, when in God's sight it is not. If, for example, you stop robbing people, they still have their money, and you don't go to jail: the results are socially good. But, if that outward change does

not involve a change of heart toward God, it creates a self-satisfied person who, to that extent, has become a Pharisee. External changes that do not follow an internal change of heart toward God always move a person further away from the Lord. So change that is socially good may be religiously evil. It is absolutely essential for the counselor to opt for change that is satisfactory to God, not merely socially good.[4]

Even in Christian circles, this biblical approach to counseling has met with stubborn resistance. Since most Christian college professors have been trained in secular universities, where secular approaches to counseling are the only ones considered, these professors prefer to adopt an integrative approach. They start with two polar positions—their personal Christian faith and their secular, scientific psychology—and then try to integrate these two into one harmonious whole. The same is characteristic of many teacher education programs conducted by Christian colleges. Also employing an integrative approach, they begin with a thoroughly secular perspective on education and then try to wed it to the Christian faith. Their results are seldom worthy of adoption, since they all fail to consult God's Word concerning His clear teachings about the nature of the people He has created. When they refuse to go back to the Author of the owner's manual, chances for success are relatively slim. Such so-called Christian counselors and Christian educators most often refuse to consider the necessity of change but look instead for simple acquisition of knowledge and personal adjustment or accommodation. Instead of going to God's Word to find the condition of the human soul, they go to their laboratories and observe the actions of mice and pigeons. Instead of seeing learning as requiring sundry kinds of personal change, they become fascinated with stimulus-response formulae and the formation of neural circuitry.

More seminaries and colleges are attempting to develop truly biblical approaches to both education and counseling. Westminster Theological Seminary, for example, promotes the Changing Lives Seminars,[5] which are designed to show God's people that there is nothing about the human heart that the Bible doesn't understand. We can change the way we think, feel, and live when we allow God to transform us through the gospel of Jesus Christ.

"The transformation of lives is at the heart of Christianity," says Gene Edward Veith, cultural affairs editor of *World*. Furthermore, he says, "At the essence of fiction is the transformation of character, how a character is changed by what happens in the story."[6] One might wish to argue the point with Veith, contending instead that the unfolding of plot is closer to the essence. After all, the unfolding of the plot is what everyone notices and what moves the story along. Veith is saying, though, that the transformation and development of character is what gives fiction its fascination. We continue reading not because of the plot but because there is a gradual, perceptible change in lives of the people who respond to the plot. Whichever literary analysis one embraces, it cannot be denied that transformation of character enriches all fiction, while a static, undeveloped character makes for dull reading.

The analogy between the world of fiction and our personal lives is often rather clear. We love fiction not because it is foreign to our own experiences but because we can see ourselves in the story. We can empathize with the character who is furiously trying to climb into the twenty-first century by learning to do e-mails before Christmas, when she doesn't have a clue as to how even to turn on the computer. We sense her intense frustration because we too have been there and have come close to dashing that stubborn machine against the wall. Why won't it perform the simplest function, when even my elementary-age grandson can make it perform all kinds of tricks? Why does it eat up letters instead of placing them on the page? Why won't the margin stay in one spot? Why does it tell me that I have just performed an illegal function when I haven't done anything unusual?

All one has to do is engage in a bit of reflective analysis in order to remember that every new learning is preceded by pain and frustration. That is why so many people begin new tasks and never finish them. That is why so many travelers buy foreign language tapes and then never listen to them. That is why so many people buy costly new books and then never read them. That is why so many college students sign up for exciting new courses and then get a drop slip before the tuition deadline has been locked in place.

All learning takes time. Learning is a process and not an act. For some types of learning, that process takes years and years. Learning to read, although composed of countless bits and pieces, takes many years before a person can claim mastery. The component segments, such as learning the sound of a short *a* or the blend of a *th*, may occur in a matter of days, thus bringing satisfaction and joy, enough to fire the next day's lesson. The completed process, however, including the ability to read critically, will take much of a lifetime.

Knowing that all learning involves a measure of pain and frustration, as well as satisfaction and success, should alert us to the fact that good teachers need patience and perseverance. Being able to sense when a student has reached his threshold of pain and frustration, and then knowing how to encourage that student to a higher level is at the heart of successful teaching. Learning to be patient, when an eighth-grade class demonstrates for the forty-second time that they have not yet mastered simple spelling rules, that is a virtue. But being persistent and not throwing in the towel is even greater.

How Shall I Resist Thee, Master?

The conference went quite well for the first two days. The ministers, all Arabic-speaking pastors from the Presbyterian Church of Egypt, were mature, delightful, intelligent, and kind people. It was a pleasure to have them in class for one hour every day, gradually learning to understand them and they me. Subconsciously they were asking, Can we trust this American? Is his theology in harmony with ours? Is it derived wholly from Scripture, or is it mixed and tainted with elements from his democratic culture? The first few days they asked some well-phrased questions designed to test my personal attitudes toward the Jewish-Arab conflict, wondering whether I would side with the Israelis or with them. My answers seemed to meet with their good pleasure, for they were delighted to know that I considered Egyptians and Arabs to be included in God's Old Testament covenant.

They were well-educated men, not only possessing theological diplomas and master of divinity degrees from an excellent Egyptian seminary but also being on the cutting edge of computer technology. Many of them had e-mail addresses and computers on which they did much of their correspondence, study, and sermon preparation. These were up-to-date ambassadors of the King.

But another instructor, who also lectured one hour a day, treated them as though they were something less. Not only insensitive to the latent hostilities between Arabs and Jews but also unaware of his own attitude of intellectual superiority, this lecturer soon found that his students were demonstrating a variety of resistance techniques.

First, he discovered that they stopped taking notes. Next, they raised an array of pointed questions, which were often put off to another time or ruled out of order. It became obvious from the pastors' body language that they differed with what the lecturer was trying to teach them. Instead of looking to him with eager anticipation, their eyes drifted to the floor. Some appeared asleep. Others glanced to classmates, subtly signaling their lack of receptivity. They were too gracious to walk out in protest or argue vociferously. As proclaimers of the gospel of peace, they had to practice what they preached. And so they applauded politely at the end of each hour before hurrying on their way only to show renewed vitality once outside the classroom. These Christians had mastered the art of respectful disagreement.

The scene that unfolded each day reminded me, by way of contrast, of some classes I had to take in high school. One in particular stands out because the change in all of our attitudes was so gradual and yet so profound. As teenagers, we had not yet learned to show respect while resisting change. We eleventh-grade students were required to take a one-semester course in music appreciation. But all we brought to the course was a fascination for 1950s jukebox music. It was what we always managed to find on our car radios and in the cafés where we gathered nightly. We loved contemporary music!

Our teacher, though, despised it and had the challenge of teaching us to love and understand classical and sacred music. She didn't put the curriculum up for a classroom referendum, for she knew that her choices would not get the popular vote. She had her own lofty tastes and was determined to change ours. Though she never actually said so, we all sensed it. The gulf between Frankie Avalon and Ludwig von Beethoven was too great not to notice. She wanted us to dump Frankie for Ludwig.

None of us clamored to make that change. None of us pleaded for longer assignments. None of us sat in the front row or stayed after class to hear one more aria from Handel's *Messiah*. On the contrary, we retreated to the back rows and corner seats where we could hide from her roving eyes. But the less enthused we were, the more animated she became. As she would explain the different symphony movements or the differences between an oboe and a clarinet, her excitement grew. Rapturous words poured out of her mouth, along with a spray of saliva that reached the front-row seats. Unfortunately, her spitting fascinated us more than her teaching. We didn't hate her, for she had built a reputation as an excellent teacher of whom our older siblings—and later we ourselves—spoke well. But, at the time, we didn't like her music, and we made that obvious. Often we would sit in silent protest, with eyes down and minds far away.

Occasionally, when she would force us to listen to her music, we would object with questions meant to trip up and humiliate her. One schemer might try to derail her train of thought, in hopes that she would talk about something else. But it seldom worked; she was too focused. Others, too smart for their own good, would memorize all the right answers for the upcoming tests while vowing inwardly never to change their personal tastes. They wanted good grades and scholarships, not enlightenment. But over time, our tastes did indeed gradually change.

What occurred in that classroom was nothing unusual. There are a multitude of ways to resist instruction, whether in the classroom, the lecture hall, business conferences, or the church. No one wants to abandon his own firmly held values. No one invites change in his life. We all are inclined to hold onto what we like, until we are persuaded that a change would be good for us. As that process of persuasion occurs, resistance breaks down bit by bit, day by day, as did our resistance to our teacher's music. Until then, absenteeism will always be a problem, for students can find a number of ways of missing school without penalty. Notes from parents can easily be forged. A mild sore throat can easily be turned into a major case of the flu before the morning bus arrives.

My parents were not so naïve as to buy my pleas; they almost always took the side of my teachers. In my elementary days one spanking from the principal resulted in two spankings from my father. I soon learned that the road of resistance could cause much pain. The road of polite acquiescence met with far fewer sanctions. I didn't have to agree with what I was taught, but I had better politely refine my modes of resistance so as to incur the least troubles. In the process, I also encountered some stinging rebukes, some even from my favorite teachers, but an even greater number from my father, who seemed to be in weekly contact with the principal. It turns out that he was, for he served on the school board with distinction for a number of terms. With home and school teaming up against me, I had little chance of winning the war.

Resistance, however, is not always the norm. Many students appear eager to learn. Is that a mirage, or do students sometimes really desire learning? Do they approach the classroom with eager anticipation, encouraging their classmates to show respect and foster a learning atmosphere? Do students who plead for quiet really want to learn?

The answer is a qualified yes. Learning, though at first painful, is also pleasant. The initial phases of any new learning experience are marked by pain, frustration, and resistance. If the learning experience is good and wholesome, however, the outcome is a real sense of joy, accomplishment, and satisfaction.

Consider, for example, the challenge of learning to ride a bicycle, mentioned earlier. The initial efforts involve intense levels of anxiety, with fear written all over the child's face as he or she tries to balance the bike, under a father's strong and steady hand. Typical children cry out in fear and insist that Father stay right there to keep them from falling. A child will also plead with Mother to take her off that dangerous contraption and stop the process. Soon, however, that painful part of the process becomes a fading memory. The negative phase begins to pass. Skills develop and success begins to occur. Now satisfaction, a sense of accomplishment, and genuine joy begin to surface. The outcome of the process is fun. Now, as children sense that satisfaction, their parents can't keep them off the bike and have to insist that the joy riding stop in time for supper. A quiet and subtle change has occurred, breaking down fearful resistance to riding and replacing it with eager anticipation.

One sure way to avoid the innate resistance that accompanies the initial phases of all significant learning is to avoid learning itself.

Some teachers, in their mad pursuit of pleasure and their desire to make the classroom fun, appeal to the students for their approach to the curriculum. What would you like to learn? is a foolish question, for the typical student wants only to avoid new learning. Augustine, that venerable saint of Roman times, describes in delightful detail how he approached the assignments of his school days. Writing his *Confessions,* he reflects thus on his boyhood days at school:

> For we feared not our torments less; nor prayed we less to Thee to escape them. And yet we sinned, in writing or reading or studying less than was expected of us. For we wanted not, O Lord, memory of capacity, whereof Thy will gave enough for our age; but our sole delight was play; and for this we were punished by those who yet themselves were doing the like. . . . O Lord, my God, I sinned in transgressing the commands of my parents and those of my masters. For what they, with whatever motive, would have me learn, I might afterwards have put to good use.
>
> For I disobeyed, not from a better choice, but from love of play, loving the pride of victory in my contests, and to have my ears tickled with lying fables, that they might itch the more. . . . I loved not study, and hated to be forced to it. Yet I was forced; and this was well done towards me, but I did not well; for unless forced, I had not learnt.[7]

8 Who Is Responsible for Educating?

My good friend is a computer whiz. He can make that electronic box of wires and processors do almost anything. I used to watch him in amazement, wondering how he knew so much, when he is almost as ancient as I. I knew enough to keep my questions to myself, but my wife stumbled in where only she would dare venture. One day, over coffee, she queried, "Where did you learn so much about the computer?"

Only a little bit surprised, he responded, "I taught myself," with more than a hint of pride in his voice. "I just learned it over the last couple years."

"But who taught you?" was her follow-up.

"Nobody! I just learned by myself."

The homely research probe was getting her nowhere, so I interjected, hoping to redirect the question. "It isn't possible to teach yourself, is it?"

With that, the whole conversation went a little sour, and my good friend built up a wall of icy silence. He was insulted, for of course he had taught himself. He knew exactly how he had acquired these skills, and he did not appreciate being challenged, even by a friend.

I wasn't trying to be obnoxious, and I wasn't trying to ruin a good friendship, but I thought that teachers and learners had to be two different persons. The more I tried to press the issue, the higher the wall went, so I soon allowed him to change the subject to something not quite so confrontational. The temperature of the coffee was our next topic.

Are Teachers Necessary?

When we had a chance for privacy, my wife raised the issue with me. "Is it really true," she asked, "that the teacher and the learner must be two separate persons? Isn't it possible for one person to teach himself something that he had not known before? Can I not teach myself how to play the piano? Can I not teach myself the facts of history? Can not a young boy who goes out into the woods all by himself learn about trees and frogs and bees?"

"The answer, my dear, is not so simple as that! In order for our good friend to learn the ways to make that computer dance and draw and sing, he had to have someone who already knew all that and who could teach it to him. He didn't see that teacher, but that does not mean that he or she was not there. What he did, and what you can do, is to take the manual that came with the computer and read it. It is organized with a clear index, and you can look up anything you want to know. If you want to learn how to copy a document from the hard drive to a disk, so that you end up with two identical sets of data in storage, all you have to do is turn in the index to 'copy' and it will give complete, detailed instructions on how to do that. If your computer is loaded with a Help menu, you can do the same thing by clicking on that icon. His method of learning is no different from that of the students who sit in school and are told by the teacher that they have to read the chapter in their math book."

"Yes, I know that, but where is Richard's teacher?"

"I don't know where he or she is physically sitting right now, but I know that person probably was sitting somewhere in Silicon Valley when he or she programmed that computer and put all those instructions into both the book and into the Help file. Some person was responsible for putting all those lessons together. That is why Dell, IBM, Gateway, and all the others need to hire so many programmers and software designers. Vast numbers of them are teachers who never have to confront their students face to face. They never have to fear rotten eggs for failed exams. They deal with students only through intermediate agencies, such as your machine. Others are hired as technical support. They do all their teaching over the phone. People who get frustrated with their equipment can call the technical support office and get all their questions answered over the telephone lines. Once their contract for free service has run out, they will have to pay the instructor some tuition, but it hardly seems like that when you just give them a credit card number."

"I think I see what you are driving at. The teacher is not there in person but uses an electronic medium and thus can do her teaching from a thousand miles and even years away. Richard didn't teach himself, as he claimed, but he was taught by someone he could not see. Is that what you are saying?"

"Precisely, dear. The answer would be no different if he had walked over to the library and picked David's psalms, Plato's dialogues, or Augustine's *City of God* off the shelf. Anyone can learn a great deal by reading such books, but it would be a little presumptuous to claim that you had taught yourself the truths contained in those classics. Even though those great teachers were not in your physical presence, it would only be a matter of ethics and courtesy to acknowledge that they had taught you through their writings. To claim their understanding of truth for yourself would be more than presumptuous. It would be a classic case of literary theft. Claiming for yourself what belongs to someone else is plagiarism. That is a pretty serious offence in our culture.

"To pursue the matter even further, consider how much one can learn by watching television, or by renting a video, or by listening to a tape. If you claim that you taught yourself everything that you had learned via these media, you would be engaged in plagiarism or electronic theft, but you would also be demonstrating an ignorance of our culture and the role that the media play in it. Those who sit in Hollywood studios and in Fifth Avenue penthouse suites control much of our intellectual diet today and do much to determine what we know and what we believe. Those who bring us the news become our teachers, deciding for us each day what they consider important and worthy of our attention. We may not like it, but those are inescapable facts, unless we bury our heads under our pillows and shut out all the media that bombard the rest of us."

"Are Bill Cosby and Peter Jennings and Oprah Winfrey then part of our national teaching staff? Are all of those who speak into mikes and smile at cameras trying to teach us something? Are they as much a teacher as is Mr. Betten in grade 2? Are John Knox, Jonathon Edwards, and Martin Luther King still teaching us from the grave? Do Dr. James Dobson and Dr. D. James Kennedy become our teachers when we buy their videos or watch them on the screen?"

"Of course! With today's communication equipment and advanced technology, we can engage in teaching others whom we have never seen or met. Many colleges and seminaries are setting up what are called distance or electronic campuses, allowing students to study at their institutions without ever leaving their families or homes. The interaction mode is still being fine-tuned, but with e-mails, Internet chat groups, and digital phones, a student in Timbuktu can interact with his instructor in Dyer almost as easily as can that young man sweating out a lecture in the presence of a flesh-and-blood professor."

"What you say is all fine and good, but what about the boy in the woods? The one I mentioned earlier."

"Yes, of course. What about him?"

"Well, I mentioned that he could go out into the woods all by himself, and there learn about trees and frogs and bees. Who is his teacher?"

"Ah, there is a difficult question. If my original challenge to Richard is valid, either this young lad has learned nothing that he had not previously known, or my assertion is false and needs to be discarded. Our options are multiple, so they must be examined quickly.

"First, we could adopt the theory of John Locke, which insists that the young lad has an empty mind, a tabula rasa, you recall, that gradually becomes filled as the environment sends out its stimuli that find receptivity in the brain. The trees and the frogs and the bees are then the sources of these stimuli, the ones from whom these signals emit. The transmission originates not with the boy but with the things from which he learns. The tree, the frog, and the bee then become his teachers, for they are the source of his knowledge."

"Oh, please, dear, do not bombard me with such nonsense. If that should be true of such living creatures, must it not also be true for what is dead or inorganic? Would not then the rocks and the road kill also become our teachers? Would not the moon, the stars, the dust, and the dirt also become our teachers? Surely that is nonsense, for if everything is a teacher, then nothing is a teacher!"

"Quite right, my dear! Let me remind you that I was not defending that proposition, just offering it as one possible explanation. Since it is the most popular on the market, I thought it best to start there."

"Yes, yes, I can understand. What other flea-brained theories do you have to offer?"

"Well, I could return to our good friend Plato. You recall that Socrates had argued in the *Republic* and in the *Phaedo* that the child is born with all innate knowledge, which is trapped in his prisonlike body. You recall too that learning is the recollection of that which was previously known."

"Yes, I remember that discussion."

"In Plato's mind, the answer is simple. The boy did not learn anything new. Before he was ever born, he knew all about trees and frogs and bees. What happened in the woods that day was a reminder of what he already knew. Seeing those creatures up close helped him recall what his soul had known from eternity.

"But there must be a better explanation, for Plato seems to suggest that the boy is omniscient from birth, that his soul at least is on a par with God. The only real purpose for living is to help his soul escape from his body. The loftiest goal is to leave this body and be reunited with the eternal Good. He might as well expedite matters and commit suicide, as did the great teacher who drank the hemlock. We might as well all join the Hemlock Society."

"Please, don't be so morbid. Is that the best you can offer?"

"No, there is a third alternative, but you may not like it. Most people don't."

"That might be, but I can't make that decision until I know what the option is. I'm waiting!"

"Well, it has to do with God, the Creator. This earth and everything in it, including the trees, the frogs, and the bees, were designed and created by none other than God. In His almighty power and wisdom, He created everything for His glory. The beauty of the mountains, the marvelous array of His creatures, the majesty of the universe, all exist for His praise. He designed everything according to His master plan. All the fish, all the birds, all the animals, and everything else are demonstrations of His marvelous creative ability. He made them not only for His own glory but also for our use and for our enjoyment."

"Yes, yes, the psalmist tells me that [see Ps. 19:1–10; Isa. 40:21–22; Rom. 1:18—3:19], but you haven't answered my question. Where is the teacher when the boy goes out into the woods by himself? Our problem won't disappear until you solve that."

"You are right, but I must first correct your question. You stated it badly, because you assumed that the boy was by himself. That is a faulty assumption, for no man is an island. No man is master of his own destiny. No man or boy exists by himself.

"Your boy could not see his teacher, any more than Richard could see his instructor for computer skills. Just because he cannot see something does not mean that the thing does not exist. Countless things are not visible to the physical eye, but they are to the eye of faith. God, you see, is his Teacher. God 'is Spirit, and those who worship Him must worship in spirit and truth' (John 4:24). Furthermore, 'do you not know that your body is the temple of the Holy Spirit who is in you, whom you have from God, and you are not your own? For you were bought at a price' (1 Cor. 6:19–20)?"

"I had almost forgotten that. What a marvelous truth. We are never alone in this world, even when boys go off into the woods to explore and play. So David was on target when he said:

> O LORD, You have searched me and known me.
> You know my sitting down and my rising up;
> You understand my thought afar off.
> You comprehend my path and my lying down,
> And are acquainted with all my ways.
> For there is not a word on my tongue,
> But behold, O LORD, You know it altogether.
> You have hedged me behind and before,
> And laid Your hand upon me.
> Such knowledge is too wonderful for me;
> It is high, I cannot attain it." (Ps. 139:1–6)

"Ah, yes. Such knowledge is too wonderful. I cannot comprehend it, but I know it is true. How else could I explain it? How else could I answer your original question?"

"Okay, your answer is marvelous, but why should Richard have turned so cold when you wouldn't accept his explanation? Why did he have to insist that he had taught himself? Why couldn't he have given God the glory? Is not the Teacher entitled to legitimate praise for His work? Why couldn't he have said, 'The Lord has revealed it to me'?"

"That would have been an excellent response, but that is not the way we are. We so easily fall prey to the sin of pride. We want to take all the credit for ourselves. It makes us sound important. It makes people praise us. It sounds great to say, 'I have taught myself. Look what I have learned!'"

"That might sound impressive, but look what happened to King Nebuchadnezzar. He looked out over his vast empire and said, 'Is not this great Babylon, that I have built for a royal dwelling by my mighty power and for the honor of my majesty?' (Dan. 4:30)."

"Yes, yes, I know the story well."

Are Home Schools Really Schools?

Springtime in Chicago is hardly a pleasant experience. Not knowing whether to welcome the daffodils or give the snowplows one last assignment, the weather fluctuates like the wind off Lake Michigan, warm one day and freezing the next. That is why most college students skip classes two days before the start of spring break and head to Florida's beaches.

I was sitting in my office on one of those blustery days, waiting for the campus to clear so I could also head south. Suddenly, without appointment, in walked a former student, now matured and holding down a principal's job in a fine Christian school hundreds of miles away. I did not expect to see him but managed to recall his name.

"Welcome, Bruce, what brings you to our windy city?"

It didn't take long to recognize that he wasn't there to pass the time away or to renew old connections. Former students who show up at professor's doors years later often have a problem to solve, a favor to ask, or an axe to grind. In this case, there was a major problem for which he sought a solution.

The Midwest town where Bruce lived was known for its long history of support for parent-controlled Christian elementary and secondary schools. Almost half of the local children attended. There was also a substantial public school system, of approximately the same size, but those were the only institutions competing for the village offspring. The law was clear, with every able-bodied child required to attend until the sixteenth birthday had been reached. Then, if anyone was so foolish, they could opt out and go to work. On the entry side, no one had to be in school until the age of seven, but no one remembered that, since almost every parent was insistent that their little ones be enrolled in kindergarten by their fifth birthday. School was almost sacred, even more so than the local churches, which were optional institutions with no civil penalty for lack of attendance.

All of that social fabric was threatening to become undone. One prominent man, a minister of the gospel, had announced that he had made plans to home school his younger children, starting the next August.

There was the reason for Bruce's visit to my office. As a professor of education, certainly I could offer some advice as to how to persuade the pastor of his erroneous thinking and stamp out the brush fire that was about to engulf his town. How could I help him load his arsenal with arguments that would convince the board of directors, the pastor's own council, and the hundreds of other parents that such defiant attitudes could not be tolerated? Everyone must be enrolled in one or the other. The threat to enroll in neither was unconscionable. To suggest that a home school could meet a child's educational needs was unthinkable. It was a rejection of the teachers' competence and of the principal's authority. To let this go would be to invite chaos in the community.

After listening carefully for some time and probing deftly for motives and possible reactions, I concluded that the best way for Bruce to respond was to offer this family as much support and assistance as he and the staff could muster. The school, after all, had long promoted itself as a "parent-controlled school, run by a society of parents." The parents had brought the school into existence not because the law required it but because they had concluded that their lives were too busy with other tasks and responsibilities for them to do the job themselves. If they had merely wanted to meet the letter of the law, there was the public school down the street, where all the tuition and fees were covered by local taxes.

Especially when dealing with recalcitrant kids, the parents often had reminded the teachers and administrators that they served *in loco parentis*. Teachers and principals had the right to apply discipline because they were acting on behalf of the parents. The concept had even been cemented into American judicial codes, with teachers and school officials never having original authority but serving only in the place of parents. At one point in American history, the state of Oregon had tried to pass a measure that made all children wards of the state, but the courts rejected such legislation.[1] Children belonged to parents and not to the state, so the state had no right to compel them to attend only public schools.

At one point in our conversation I had to remind Bruce that he and almost every other administrator had probably argued for smaller class sizes in his school. Had he not presented the teachers' arguments that smaller classes meant better instruction? Had he not pleaded for teacher aides so that more students could get individualized help? What could be better than having a gifted teacher with only three students in her class all day? How much more personalized could it get?

When I inquired about the qualifications of the mother, who was going to do the bulk of the teaching, Bruce had to admit that she was fully certified by the state and had graduated from a reputable teacher education program. She had been a regular classroom teacher until her own children's needs persuaded her to give up her professional career. What could be wrong with letting her teach her own children in the confines of her own home?

That dialogue in the latter part of the 1980s was not joyfully accepted, but it was enough to persuade Bruce that he should not go home and wage war with the pastor. It didn't convince him that home schooling was a great idea and should be endorsed. In his mind, the issue was largely financial. Parents, he was convinced, did not want to pay the escalating tuition costs to the Christian school and were too proud to ask the deacons at church for assistance. The battle was just beginning, he insisted, but he would sit on the sidelines this time and watch for the outcome. If the education department of his favorite college would not support and equip him, what point would there be in a major skirmish?

In less than two decades, the scene has changed remarkably. For years and years, there were some intense legal and political battles, with many parents being fined and charged with civil disobedience.[2] Agencies such as the Home School Legal Defense Fund (HSLDF) rose up to provide the legal assistance and mountains of research evidence to help those beleaguered parents. There was a long period of intense confrontation, with increasing numbers of parents refusing to enroll their children in what were considered the only schools in town. Parents insisted that the family room in their home also qualified as a school. It had everything that was essential to good education: able students, a qualified teacher, an approved curriculum, clean bathrooms, and a safe playground near by. Furthermore, it had the closest and most desired parental support that any school could ever desire. On top of that, it made no demands on the tax base. What more could be desired? What else was required?

Since then, in almost every state of the union, the battle for home schools has been won. The time of confrontation has passed. The era of cooperation has begun. Federal and state agencies have recognized the legitimacy of home schools and have even mandated cooperation for those administrative districts that prefer to continue the battle. Countless support groups have sprung up, providing curricular resources in almost every conceivable subject area. Colleges and universities have welcomed home-schooled students with generous scholarships, often earned on the basis of outstanding academic achievement.

Home schools have now become an accepted part of the educational network, with millions of children legally enrolled as students in their own homes. No longer must every student across the land be in a classroom with twenty-five other students all the same age in a militaristic type of monopoly controlled by unions of so-called professionals. No longer does everyone have to bow blindly before the myth that bigger is better, for the littlest schools in the land have often outshone those consolidated behemoths run by the state.

The battle for acceptance has been won. But the battle about quality will go on and on. Just because a school is small is no guarantee that it is good. Just because a loving mother or a caring father is doing the bulk of the teaching is no assurance that the quality of education will be superb. The quality of learning is always conditioned by the quality of the teaching. Since teachers are still essential, those who would teach the children whom our heavenly Father has entrusted to their care will always need to measure their efforts against the standards of that Father's manual for instruction. Are their priorities in line with His? Are their objectives based on His Word? Are their outcomes showing daily signs of being transformed into that good and acceptable and perfect will of God?

Over the past few years, I have had the privilege of going into many homes as part of my pastoral duties. In the communities that I serve, more and more families are setting up home schools. Whenever there are children present, I have tried to engage them in the conversation. My opening question is often whether or not they like school. If the answer is in the negative, I try to probe what lies behind that dissatisfaction. If it is positive, I follow that with a question of whether they like their teacher. At that point there is a strange set of giggles around the table, with furtive glances between the children and their mother. The answer almost always comes out with an enthusiastic yes. The mother breathes a big sigh of relief, and we go on.

When kids love their teacher and when kids love their schooling, the road to success is well paved. With large, conventional schools, the answer to my queries is often negative. There is a natural inclination to dislike the rigors of schooling, especially when the teacher is judged unfavorably. In the impersonal, secular, professional public systems where the majority of students are mandated to attend, there is growing evidence that the teachers have become the enemies of many students. That is one indication of bankrupt conditions.

When it became apparent that the home school movement would not ruin their monopoly, the National Education Association (NEA) and the American Federation of Teachers (AFT)[3] began looking for more dangerous enemies. The real threats, they concluded, are the new tuition vouchers that might find their way to private and even religious schools. There lies a visible threat to the only established church in the land, the church where secular humanism reigns supreme. There is a war worthy of being fought to the death.

——— 9 Implementing the Program

Dare to Discipline[1]

The incident occurred more than thirty-five years ago, yet I can remember it in vivid detail. Our oldest son had just started kindergarten. During the spring of that year he had a young friend, slightly older than he, staying with us for the weekend. On Sunday afternoon, after the meal, the two boys begged to go outside to play. Since the weather was pleasant and there didn't seem to be any wisdom in forcing them to play under our feet, we granted them permission, but not without a stern warning.

Not more than a block from the house was a deserted pond full of croaking frogs. Because of its depth and the current water temperature, it represented a legitimate danger, so I warned them not to go anywhere near it. If they did, I threatened, they would get a spanking from me.

An hour or so later the boys had disappeared from the back yard and were nowhere to be seen. I called their names a few times but got no response. Finally, with real concern for their safety, I headed toward the pond, following the easiest but not the most direct route. When I got to the pond, there was no sign of them, so I went back toward the house. There were two little boys pretending to be playing in the back yard.

The first interrogation produced only some ill-disguised lies. I could see from their shoes, with clay from the pond's perimeter clinging to them, and their pants, covered with sandburs, that they had obviously been near the pond. Finally, after I pressed the issue and pointed to the evidence that they were carrying into my backyard courthouse, they confessed.

True to my promise, I took our son into the house, marched him into his bedroom, laid him across my knees, and gave him a pretty stiff paddling, enough to make him cry loudly. Then, laying him on his bed, I told him that he could come out of his room when he was ready to talk to me about his disobedient behavior. He lay there sobbing, and I left.

Reappearing in the living room, I found that his friend was sitting there waiting. Much to my surprise, he asked, "Do I get one, too?"

I thought for a couple of seconds, but it seemed like an eternity. What should I say? Should I grant him his wish, for that is what it was? What would his parents say, for they would certainly hear about it? A guest in my house, no less. Should I tell him that he would have to get that from his parents? That would not fly, however, for he knew as well as I that his parents would never spank him. They made that plain on many previous occasions.

If he were to get the spanking that he requested, he would have to get it from me. After all, I was the one who had made the promise. Having come to that decision, I took him into our bedroom, laid him across my knees, and gave him an almost equally severe spanking. He too cried, for punishments have to hurt in order to meet their own definition. Then, trying to be fair, I told him that he could come out when he was ready to talk about his disobedience.

It wasn't long before our eldest came out of his room and sauntered up to me, eyes downcast, and looking genuinely remorseful. He began with a confession of guilt, not only for disobeying the strict orders but also for lying. After a brief discussion of the seriousness of his behavior, I sent him on his way with an assurance that I had forgiven him.

Within a short time, the friend also came out of our room. Looking fully as penitent as had my son, he slowly approached me and then said, "Thank you. Thank you for spanking me. I am sorry I disobeyed you." It wasn't exuberant, but it was genuine. He had thanked me for paddling him! That unexpected response reminded me of the words of Hebrews 12:5–8:

My son, do not despise the chastening of the Lord,
Nor be discouraged when you are rebuked by Him;
For whom the Lord loves He chastens,
And scourges every son whom He receives.

If you endure chastening, God deals with you as with sons; for what son is there whom a father does not chasten? But if you are without chastening, of which all have become partakers, then you are illegitimate and not sons.

The writer of Hebrews reminds us that in Roman culture many rich men in the noble class had mistresses in addition to their wives. These mistresses often produced illegitimate children who were financially provided for but who were not treated the same as the sons of the noble's wife. The one who was to carry on the family name and who was to be given the inheritance was not only provided for financially but also had to undergo a rigorous regimen of training or discipline, because this was the heir, the real son. The one who would carry on the family name needed special training and education. The others had no legal standing and no love.

The young visitor in our house that spring day wanted to be treated like a son and not like an illegitimate child. Because his adoptive parents never spanked him, he felt as if he didn't really belong. Millions of kids, like those in Columbine High School, are coming to the conclusion that they don't belong either because their parents don't care for them as heirs but treat them almost as illegitimate aliens. With increasing numbers of absentee parents and dysfunctional homes, countless kids in our inner cities are looking for organizations or bodies to which they can belong. The gangs offer that sense of belonging for many. All kids, in spite of their protestations to the contrary, need to be treated as real sons and real daughters. They need to be loved. They need discipline. If they can't get discipline at home, they will find it elsewhere.

The Stubborn Resistance

For fear that this young boy might tell his parents a somewhat skewed version of this spanking incident, my wife and I promptly told them what had happened when they came to pick up their son.[2] True to our expectations, these parents were not overjoyed with our action, but neither did they protest too loudly. They, like millions of others, no longer believe in spanking or discipline. The emergence of child psychology courses, based almost always on John Locke's tabula rasa model, has convinced countless parents and teachers that spanking and punishment are old-fashioned, out of date, and erroneous.

Contrary to conventional wisdom, the One who has created children and entrusted them to our care is specific about the necessity and wisdom of spanking. In His Holy Word He instructs us,

> He who spares his rod hates his son,
> But he who loves him disciplines him promptly. (Prov. 13:24)

> Chasten your son while there is hope,
> And do not set your heart on his destruction. (Prov. 19:18)

Furthermore,

> Foolishness is bound up in the heart of a child;
> The rod of correction will drive it far from him. (Prov. 22:15)

> Do not withhold correction from a child,
> For if you beat him with a rod, he will not die. (Prov. 23:13)

Such language, although it is contained in the wisdom section of the Bible, has become anathema to millions of Americans. The mood is such that parents can be jailed or have their children taken away if they are seen spanking them in public. Stories abound of well-meaning parents who appropriately spank a child in the supermarket or some other public facility and then are interrogated by the county welfare worker. In the public school the situation is even worse. Teachers and principals do not dare to exercise any kind of corporal punishment for fear of losing their jobs or being sued for assault and battery. In many states, spanking has been made a criminal action. In many districts, it is not permissible for teachers to touch or hug a student on the grounds that all touching could be construed as physical abuse. Consequently students, who need so badly to be loved and embraced, are being deprived of the very signals they crave.

The anti-Christian element in society considers itself far superior to the Bible. That ancient book, they claim, could not know as much about child rearing as we do. They forget, however, that God not only condones but also requires spanking, or using the rod, as a way of showing love to sinful and emotionally starved children. Not unlike Adam and Eve, these modern experts think they know better.

In spite of such clear biblical teaching, the American Academy of Pediatrics recently published an article in which it insisted that "spanking teaches children aggression and is no more effective than other forms of punishment."[3] As a terrible substitute for discipline, more and more pediatricians are prescribing the drug Ritalin as a means of curbing and controlling undesirable behavior. According to a survey by the International Narcotics Control Board, 10 percent of all boys in the U.S. between the ages of six and fourteen are on the drug.[4]

The situation in the churches of the Western world is not much different. Except for some denominations that want to maintain orthodoxy, many churches are unwilling to practice ecclesiastical discipline. One of the marks of the true church, according to the words of the Belgic Confession of Faith, is that "it practices church discipline for correcting faults. In short, it governs itself according to the pure Word of God" (art. 29). The Westminster Confession of Faith says that

> condemnation by the church is necessary in order to reclaim and regain spiritual brothers who have committed some serious offense; to deter others from committing similar offenses; to purge that leaven which might contaminate the whole lump; to vindicate the honor of Christ and the holy profession of the gospel; and to avoid the wrath of God, which might justly fall on the church, should it allow His covenant and the sacraments to be profaned by notorious and obstinate offenders (30.3).

According to a number of surveys by the Gallup polling organization over the past decades, the primary concern of parents, when questioned about their schools, is the lack of effective discipline. At the same time, surveys aimed at determining why young teachers leave the profession after the first year clearly indicate that 80 percent of the certified teachers cite inability to control student behavior as their primary reason.

As in Plato's beloved Athens, the spirit of democracy has invaded the churches as well as the schools. It is as though there is a maddening desire to sing, "What glorious freedoms abound, when everyone does what is right in his own eyes!"

This deplorable state of affairs is the result of wholesale ignorance. When confronted, most antidisciplinarians insist that nobody in his right mind wants to discipline. When they are asked why, they retort that the word means "to punish." If you love, they insist, you must show love and not anger. In fact, said B. F. Skinner, punishment is counterproductive. It increases disobedience and misbehavior. Church leaders follow that same line of reasoning, insisting that ecclesiastical decisions of censure and excommunication drive people away from the church and give it a bad name. Instead, they argue, the elders must embrace and encourage those who have sinned.

If discipline were defined as punishment, then I would also be less inclined to endorse it. But that is not what the word has historically meant. The word *discipline* derives from the root word *disciple*, which is a synonym for student or learner. The word in Latin was *discipulus*, meaning "one who receives instructions." Jesus used that same word in the Great Commission when He instructed His disciples, "Go therefore and make disciples of all the nations" (Matt. 28:19). The words that Hebrews uses in the passage cited earlier are variations of the Greek word *paideia*, which means "education," "training," or "correction"; in the verb form the word means "to correct," "to teach," "to instruct," or "to train." The pedagogue is the teacher, the one who brings about instruction.

When a standard English dictionary is consulted, the reader will find that there are usually five different meanings given to the word. For the noun, the five meanings, in order of citation, are

(1) instruction, teaching;
(2) any branch of knowledge (e.g., history, mathematics, biology);

(3) training that molds, corrects, or perfects;
(4) punishment;
(5) controlled behavior gained by the preceding.

Whenever I broached the subject in my teacher training classes, students would almost inevitably put punishment as the first definition. They were surprised to find that it rightfully belonged in the fourth spot. The logic involved is simple and is reinforced by the definitions given for the verb form. According to those same dictionaries, the verb *discipline* has two meanings:

(1) to teach, to instruct;
(2) to punish.

The whole purpose of education, whether at home, at school, or at church, is to teach the recipient some important truth, behavior, attitude, or skill. The tools that we use for that instruction are called disciplines or subjects, also called curriculum. By repeated use of those tools, we aim to develop or train for a particular kind of result or outcome that shapes, corrects, or perfects that person's character and performance. When that effort proves to be unsuccessful, we must then punish the wrong behavior with sufficient severity that the desired behavior is attained. When that is finally accomplished, often after many years of persistent and patient effort, we then can look at the student and see that he or she has truly acquired the behavior or skill that we were seeking.

If *Webster's New Collegiate Dictionary* is correct, then discipline is teaching and teaching is discipline. By the laws of mathematics, it is correct to say that good teaching is good discipline and good discipline is good teaching. It is equally correct to insist that bad discipline is bad teaching.

To not punish at the point of resistance is to give up, to declare the effort a failure, and thus to ensure that it will truly be a failure. To decide that punishment is evil is to declare that you don't have the heart to be a teacher. The best thing then is to leave the profession and find some job where the responsibility and the rewards are far less. To dare to discipline is to dare to teach.

The Consequences of Discipline

The writer of Hebrews reminds us that "no chastening seems to be joyful for the present, but grievous ["painful," NIV]; nevertheless, afterward it yields the peaceable fruit of righteousness to those who have been trained by it" (Heb. 12:11). In addition, he says, "We may be partakers of [God's] holiness" (v. 10). The holiness of God consists in His mind and will being in perfect harmony with truth and righteousness. To become "partakers in His holiness" is to have our minds, our wills, and our desires brought into perfect harmony with God's mind. Using the argument from the lesser to the greater, we can see what happens in this life between fathers and their children. For a long time, during the formative years, there are sometimes intense friction and confrontation between a father and his children, with the children unwilling to accept the father's values, his faith, his code of conduct, his way of living. Finally, after years of tension and tugging, the children begin to recognize that Dad was right all along, that Father knew best, and that their greatest joy would be in accepting his rule as best for themselves.

As God the Holy Spirit transforms us by the daily renewing of our minds and through the sufferings and refinements of this life, we begin to enter into the joy of Jesus Christ, to think as He thinks, and to live the way He wants us to. Good discipline will also produce a harvest of peace. Sin brings misery into our lives, but discipline brings joy and satisfaction. The great transforming process, in which chastisement holds an important place, will keep on working its will in our lives until we become completely righteous and holy and love only the things that God loves.

At the time we are going through this refining process, no one should be so foolish as to claim that it is fun, pleasant, or enjoyable. The text tells us that "no discipline seems pleasant at the time, but painful" (v. 11). "Later on, however, it produces a harvest of righteousness and peace for those who have been trained by it" (Heb. 12:11 NIV).

Taking Thoughts Captive to Christ

Every summer, when we contemplate the excitement of starting another school year and wonder aloud how we are going to pay off the tuition account, the necessity of Christian schools again begins to nag us. Are Christian schools worth the cost of tuition? Is there enough difference between Christian and secular education to pay hundreds of dollars in tuition every month?

In order to answer such questions with any sense of finality, we have to dig deep into fundamental questions about the character and the primary purposes of the Christian schools we have established. Oftentimes we turn to Proverbs 22:6 for answers and find the adamant reminder to "train up a child in the way he should go, and when he is old he will not depart from it." This classic passage is worthy of our attention and should continue to spur us on for many generations to come, but it is not the only text that should be used to justify Christian education.

Let me suggest another that is not so transparent, but one that I think is rich with meaning and insight. In Paul's second letter to the church at Corinth, he defends his oftentimes controversial ministry with these words: "For the weapons of our warfare are not carnal but mighty in God for pulling down strongholds, casting down arguments and every high thing that exalts itself against the knowledge of God, bringing every thought into captivity to the obedience of Christ" (2 Cor. 10:4–5).

When we take a look at this verse in the Bible, we can focus on any one of the words or phrases the apostle Paul used here. Depending on which word or phrase we begin with, we could give a different spin or twist to the intended meaning. If we start at the beginning of Paul's statement, we notice that he is assuming a condition of warfare. Paul does not defend that thesis, for he assumes that his readers find it to be self-evident. We don't live in a peaceful, neutral kind of society, where people are eager to live at peace and are concerned about each other's welfare. Far from it. We live, says Paul, where conflict is self-evident. We may not experience the level of physical violence experienced in Belfast, Northern Ireland, or in the West Bank of Israel, but there is war nonetheless. Those who live out of allegiance to the devil do everything conceivable to attack those who follow Jesus Christ. Those who hate God also hate His disciples. Those who live for self or Satan will do everything to entice others into their lifestyle.

Those who are in love with feminism, with the homosexual

agenda, with the gambling industry, with the sexual revolution, with pornography, with abortion, with evolution, with the drug culture, and any other sin that besets our culture are unwilling to let the opposition enjoy any tranquility. On the contrary, those controlled by these horrible evils are constantly seeking whom they may persuade to join their cause. The day that they persuade us that we live in a peaceful, neutral society will be the day that they have lulled us to sleep. The day that we think that public education is neutral will be the day that we die spiritually. Nothing could be further from the truth.

The Knowledge of God

To catch the full import of what Paul is writing to the Corinthians, we would do well to start our probe with the phrase "the knowledge of God," for we ought always to start and to end with God. The knowledge of God is difficult enough to comprehend, for that little preposition *of* can mean either "about" or "belonging to." If we are talking about the knowledge that we may have about God, we will limit our studies to the area of theology, which is defined as the study about God. If we choose the other preposition, namely, the "of" that connotes ownership, we are asking a far broader question and one that may be more difficult to answer.

I am convinced that in this passage the phrase "the knowledge of God" can and should be defined both ways, addressing then the questions about the knowledge that belongs to God. It is with the second question that we will concern ourselves primarily. When we address this second question about which knowledge belongs to God, we must confess at the outset that God obviously has knowledge of everything He created. He knows intimately everything He has made, and thus He has knowledge of everything.

David expresses that truth powerfully and pointedly when he writes:

> O LORD, You have searched me and known me,
> You know my sitting down and my rising up;
> You understand my thought afar off.
> You comprehend my path and my lying down,

And are acquainted with all my ways.
For there is not a word on my tongue,
But behold, O LORD, You know it altogether.
You have hedged me behind and before,
And laid Your hand upon me.
Such knowledge is too wonderful for me;
It is high, I cannot attain it. (Ps. 139:1–6)

When we begin to comprehend those truths and realize that God is so great that He knows our every thought—He knows our every word, even before we utter it from our lips, and He even puts words into our mouths so that we don't say the wrong thing at the wrong time—then we marvel along with the psalmist.

One of our first concerns, therefore, about the knowledge of God is its dimension or its boundaries. The Belgic Confession then leads us to two significant terms common to the Reformed faith:

1. *General revelation.* When we study the contents of either the Belgic Confession of Faith or the Westminster Confession of Faith, we find that "we know God by two means: first, by the creation, preservation, and government of the universe; which is before our eyes as a most elegant book, wherein all creatures, great and small, are as so many characters leading us to see clearly the invisible things of God" (Belgic Confession, art. 2). When we think of the magnitude of general revelation, we are thinking of everything outside of the Bible itself. The entire universe, including the farthest stars, the largest trees, the tiniest insects, the prettiest flowers, and all things or persons that God has created are part of that general revelation.

When we think of our school curriculum, we need to put all of the subjects, except the Bible, within that category. We then have to acknowledge that history, mathematics, physics, art, Spanish, book-keeping, English, basketball, tennis, and biology are all a part of general revelation. None of our school subjects are outside that category.

We also do well to remember that God's world, the vast universe that He created, is not a veil or mask designed to hide the Creator's power and majesty. On the contrary, "the heavens declare the glory of God; and the firmament shows His handiwork" (Ps. 19:1). Everywhere we look in the world around us we see evidences that there is a mighty and marvelous Creator. The proofs for intelligent design are so numerous as to leave all of us without excuse.

General revelation is not always the most easily understood term, but it is so called because it comes to everyone, just through our being alive in God's world. God has revealed Himself this way from the start of human history. He actively discloses these aspects of Himself to everyone, whether that person is living in the inner city of Chicago, in the gutters of Calcutta, in the mountains of Peru, on a lake at Howard City, or on a farm in Iowa.

2. *Special revelation.* Our confession is explicit in telling us that any and all of the categories of general revelation are sufficient to convince men that there is truly a God and to leave them without excuse, "yet they are not sufficient to give that knowledge of God, and of His will, which is necessary unto salvation" (Westminster Confession of Faith, chap. 1). In order to give that knowledge of God necessary unto salvation, God "makes Himself more clearly and fully known to us by His holy and divine Word, that is to say, as far as is necessary for us to know in this life, to His glory and our salvation" (Belgic Confession, chap. 2). As a primary means of grace, God has chosen to give us His Word, to give us the abilities to read it, to translate it into hundreds of different languages, and to comprehend its meanings.

But there is another way by which we have the knowledge of God. Technically it is not separate from the preceding two categories, so we should think of it as one of the dimensions of general revelation, on the grounds that it is a part of God's created order. It is contained within us, as the crown of creation, but is so special that we need to focus on it separately for a moment.

One of the most amazing aspects of the way in which God has created us is the fact that we are born with a conscience. We come into the world with "the law of God written on our hearts." From the day that we are born, we know right from wrong. We don't need to have our parents tell us that it is wrong to steal or wrong to punch our little sister or wrong to tell lies. We know when we do evil because God created us with that capacity. Adam and Eve were created with perfect righteousness and perfect holiness. But they felt guilty as soon as they disobeyed God's commands, so they went off to hide themselves and to cover their nakedness with fig leaves.

Even in the fallen world all people are endowed with a conscience that condemns them, telling them that they ought to suffer for wrongs that they have done. "Conscience" comes from two words, *con*, or "with," and *science*, or "knowledge." We are created with knowledge of what is right and what is wrong. When we go against that knowledge, contrary to what we know is right, we suffer the pangs or jabs of that conscience, telling us that we should not do that again.

The Source of Knowledge

We all have to recognize that there is a great deal of knowledge around us and available to us. We can take a look at our libraries ("media centers" is a more current phrase) and stand in awe of the millions of books that have been written, of the hundreds of thousands of movies and videos that have been made, of the scores and scores of software programs for our computers. Where does it all come from?

Our secular culture has a variety of answers, many of which have come down to us through history. Some philosophers such as Immanuel Kant and John Dewey have argued that all knowledge is experiential, that we can come to know only what we have experienced. They would even argue that we cannot know God (i.e., know about God), because He is not experiential; He is not in the category of the phenomenal. Others, like John Locke and Jean Jacques Rousseau, have argued that all knowledge comes to us from our environment, that the material things of this world radiate knowledge from themselves, and that we are a passive sponge that absorbs what we can. We have no conscience at birth and no original sin, but only a blank slate. We are only what we become, what our environmental influences make us to be, they claim. In the words of Dewey, we are "social resultants," products of our culture, nothing more.

There are also vast numbers of people who would like to have us believe that science is the source of knowledge. Only as we put our faith in science, they claim, can we hope to increase our knowledge and someday come to knowledge of the truth. Such belief is rank heresy and can be demolished (to borrow Paul's term) at the most fundamental level by pointing out that science is nothing more than a synonym for knowledge, thus leaving us with the indefensible hypothesis that knowledge is its own source, that it is self-generating.

When the Bible talks about the knowledge of God, it is talking about the knowledge that belongs to God and that comes from Him. It belongs to God because He is the source. All knowledge, whether it is the knowledge of arithmetic, or of biology, or of music, or of chemistry, or any other study, comes from Him and from nowhere else

The Character of Knowledge

What we have to recognize from all of our foregoing discussion is that all knowledge is revelation. When we put all knowledge into the two categories, general and special revelation, we have to come to recognize that everything is revelation. To make that claim is to admit that it does not originate in discovery or rational deduction or scientific experiment. If we read the conventional textbooks of teaching and learning theory, we would never get the impression from them that knowledge has anything to do with revelation. As a matter of conviction, they would refuse to allow such terminology into their textbooks, for revelation suggests strongly that knowledge comes, gift-fashion, from somewhere outside of ourselves. To admit that knowledge comes to us by revelation is to drag religion into the classroom. Perish the thought!

Learning theorists, who give us conventional wisdom, are much more inclined to talk of knowledge in terms of discovery or rational deduction or scientific experiment. Knowledge, the secularist claims, is something that we acquire for ourselves. If we happen to possess any significant amounts, we and we alone should get all of the credit. Autonomous man loves to claim, "I am the source of all wisdom. Look what I got for myself! Look how smart I am!"

We have learned long ago, in the language of the Westminster Shorter Catechism, that "the chief end of man is to glorify God and to enjoy Him forever" (Q. 1). God gives us knowledge not so that we may puff out our chests and brag about our intelligence or our scholarships but that we may be His servants, know Him, glorify Him, and enjoy Him forever. This world exists for God's glory, not ours. In the words of Herman Bavinck, "The purpose of God's revelation according to Scriptures is this very thing: that man shall learn to know God, and hence may have eternal life."[5]

The Strategies of God's Enemies

We all know that the world is not a friend to grace and that there are enemies of God all around us. Claiming to be autonomous, that is, self-ruling, these enemies set themselves up to take God's place. Not wanting to acknowledge the sovereignty of God, they "suppress the truth in unrighteousness" (Rom. 1:18). It is not a matter of the truth being sought but hard to find. Rather, people have the truth and know the truth but deliberately suppress it so as to prevent it from being seen or heard. Anyone who has tried to have a spiritual truth published in the secular press knows how that suppression of truth works. What the Bible says "is clearly seen" fallen humanity obstructs so that its influence cannot be felt. Because they "suppress the truth in unrighteousness," they are without excuse and will have to answer some day for their obstructionist tactics.

The apostle Paul, who had his share of encounters with the enemies of the gospel, goes on to tell us, "They exchanged the truth of God for a lie, and worshiped and served created things rather than the Creator" (Rom. 1:25 NIV). A lie is a distortion or perversion of the truth and is attributable to the work of Satan rather than to the Holy Spirit. God gives us only true knowledge, but Satan takes and twists and distorts that knowledge in such a way that God is no longer given the credit or the glory.

Whenever we think we can operate apart from God or whenever we let Satan get control in our lives, we suppress the truth and swallow the lie. Whenever we think that we have acquired knowledge by our own ingenuity, we are giving credit to ourselves and taking it away from God. At that point we would do well to remember the story about Nebuchadnezzar, who had been warned by God through a dream that he had to learn the principle that "the Most High rules in the kingdom of men, gives it to whomever He will, and sets over it the lowest of men" (Dan. 4:17). Not willing to learn that profound lesson, the king marched up to the roof of his royal palace, surveyed all the buildings, and pronounced, "Is not this great Babylon, that I have built for a royal dwelling by my mighty power?" (Dan. 4:30). God heard, and God responded with a swift punishment. Such language is idolatry, says Paul. Whenever we buy into the idea that knowledge comes as a result of our effort or of scientific activity, or that science is somehow the source of knowledge, we are engaging in idolatry. We do the same if we think that truth is discovery or the product of human reason. Harsh though it may sound, we have to realize that religious honor cannot be given to any of God's creations without taking it away—in a disgraceful and sacrilegious manner—from God Himself.

The Obligations of God's Children

In light of the preceding, what are we as Christians supposed to do? What should our children, as students who are learning to find their way in this world, be taught to do? Borrowing again the language of Paul, we "cast down arguments and every high thing." Paul is reminding us here that the "wisdom of this world" is foolishness in God's sight. He is also saying that the wisdom of men must be brought low, that the secular and atheistic answers of this world must be demolished. That is strong language, but we need to remember that the kingdom of Christ cannot be set up or established until we first tear down everything in the world that is in opposition to it. Nothing is more opposed to the spiritual wisdom of God than is the "wisdom of this world"; nothing is more at variance with the glory of God than is the human attempt to put man on God's throne, to give man credit for things that God gives to him.

William Barclay gives us a translation of this passage that captures in contemporary language the thoughts that Paul was conveying. Barclay translates: "Our campaign is such that we can destroy plausible fallacies and all the lofty-mindedness which raises itself up against the knowledge that God has given."[6] To illustrate, let us take one contemporary example of a thought or an idea that has been raised up against the knowledge that God has given. I think of the common and passionately held assertion that the earth on which we live is millions or even billions of years old. The vast majority of Americans hold this to be a self-evident truth, even though the Bible, as God's special, corrective revelation, strongly suggests that we live on a young earth.

Paul says that we are to "take captive every thought." At first such language may seem strange, but he is obviously continuing the theme of warfare suggested earlier. The term *captive* is borrowed from military figures and suggests that when we demolish arguments or tear down every pretension that sets itself up against the knowledge of God, we are going to have ideas or thoughts that must be taken captive. When we encounter an idea like the ones about an old earth, we are to capture that thought and bring it, in captivity, to Jesus Christ, who is the Captain of the Lord's army in this spiritual warfare. To put it simply, we have to come with that idea and measure it against the Word of God. Does it harmonize with Scripture, or does it contradict what God is saying in His Word? Can I find the idea of an earth that is billions and billions of years old to be in agreement with all of the genealogies of Adam and of Jesus Christ given for us in Genesis 5 and 11, 1 Chronicles 1, Matthew 1, and Luke 3?

In the work that we call Christian education, we are to take every thought and "make it obedient to Christ." When we have taken ideas and measured them against the standards of the Word of God, we cannot stop there if we find an apparent contradiction. In this spiritual battle for the souls of men there are to be no draws or declarations of neutrality. We may not rest with such a conflict. Because all knowledge belongs to God and comes from Him, we must make every thought obedient to Jesus Christ. We must recapture ideas and thoughts that have been pirated by the world and bring them back into captivity to Christ. That is the task of Christian parents and Christian teachers and Christian school administrators and board members. We may never concede a square inch of God's world to the clutches of Satan, but we must demolish arguments and every false assertion that sets itself up against the knowledge of God, take those thoughts as captives, and bring them into submission to Jesus Christ, the King of the universe.

───10 Who Will Teach Reformed Doctrine?

O ne of the Christian colleges close to our home has frequently found itself on the front pages of area newspapers. Recently there were some well-documented stories about a huge beer bust in an empty field, with dozens of kegs being quaffed and numerous students brought home drunk. That kind of publicity is not helpful to the donor base, but the thinking is that boys will be boys, so why not let this pass and get on with the real business of educating. So went the spin to the constituency.

For much of the previous year there was a religious feud on this campus that was even more fodder for the press. The college's mission has been defined as that of offering "excellent, liberal-arts academic programs in the context of the 'historic Christian faith.'"[1] What that means and how that comes to expression has become a point of intense debate not only among students but also among supporters, faculty, and staff. Touching off the firestorm of protest at this college, as it has at so many others around the world, are the attitudes expressed toward homosexuals. At this institution, a courageous college chaplain invited a speaker who argued in a chapel exercise that a homosexual's orientation could be changed through repentance and faith. This message, which is anathema to gay and lesbian activists, coupled with issues of scriptural interpretation and religious pluralism, combined to create a deep rift within the institution.

One student expressed the viewpoint of the majority by declaring, "Even though we are a historic, Christian faith-based college, we are a liberal arts institution. It's necessary to have all viewpoints."[2] According to this student and a majority of the faculty, there must be a measure of tolerance and acceptance for gays and diverse religious groups. For these advocates of toleration, there was no longer any point in going to chapel "because Christianity is too narrowly presented and too many students have a my-way-or-the-highway view." This same student, a religion major, said, "I like the fact that [this college] is Christian-based, but I feel there has been a movement to make it specifically and wholly Christian. I don't agree with that!"[3]

Such statements make one wonder about the commitments of the speaker. What could be bad or wrong about a college becoming "wholly Christian"? Would it be better if it stayed "nominally" Christian? Is that akin to being partially Christian and partially pagan? Is such a desire an indication that the speaker is unwilling to submit his life to Jesus Christ but wants to maintain control over his own beliefs and choose only the commands he would like to obey? Would such an attitude of half-submission ever pass muster with Alcoholics Anonymous? Do they believe in partial submission?

When a number of Muslim students on this same campus insisted on their own prayer room, they were granted that, all on the premise that toleration trumps orthodoxy. Those who reject Jesus Christ and who substitute Muhammad as their savior have equal place on this campus. How democratic!

Tensions between Toleration and Orthodoxy

The tension between toleration and orthodoxy has reached a breaking point in many churches, schools, colleges, and seminaries. The issue came to pointed expression at a recent convention of Christian school leaders. Someone who had been nurtured in the Reformed faith asked, "Who is teaching Reformed doctrine to our children?" The question stirred a rather animated set of responses, most of which could be summarized as follows: "No one is, and no one better start!" To try to foist a particular set of religious beliefs on young, defenseless, gullible children is an affront to our democratic principles. That may have been done in your generation, but we don't want it repeated in ours. Toleration reigns. Orthodoxy dies.

Decades ago, when I was still a student at the high school and college levels, there were required courses that we dubbed "Ref Doc," an abbreviation for Reformed doctrine. Our schools and our churches were unashamedly Reformed. They required, as a matter of course, that we come to understand, appreciate, and commit to the Reformed faith. It was articulated for us in the Heidelberg Catechism, the Belgic Confession, the Canons of Dort, the Westminster Standards, and a host of other creeds and books. The name of John Calvin we bore with honor, distinction, and pride. We read the same Bible he did and saw the same truths etched on its pages. We all assumed that was the standard way to proceed, for the Baptists were just as intent on the distinctives of their schools, as were the Methodists, the Roman Catholics, and the Lutherans. That was the universally accepted modus operandi. Because of that, our choice of college was clear. We went to the school that preached the same faith as did our churches and our homes. Life was simple and sweet.

Sometime over the past three decades the character of our religious communities has subtly but radically changed. The forces bringing about these changes have a variety of hues, including modes of transportation, marriage patterns, tuition hikes, and scholarship restrictions. Most of all, our institutions have been bombarded with the assumptions of democracy, which insist that all people possess equal authority, and that the majority rules. All of these are antithetical to the kingdom of God taught so emphatically on the pages of Holy Writ, but who is to argue against democracy?[4]

Today it is difficult to find teachers in our Christian schools and officers in our church councils who know in substantive ways what it means to be Reformed or what is distinctive about historic Calvinism. These schools, colleges, and churches profess to be unashamedly Christian, but there seems to have crept in a generic brand of evangelicalism. This generic Christianity, while it speaks animatedly about outreach and missions, becomes more and more shallow in its understanding of doctrine of any kind. Creeds have been left to collect dust in the back rooms, with catechism and confirmation classes confined to the scrap heaps of history.

There is in many quarters a hyperkinetic effort at bringing people into the church, while those same churches offer less and less to those who come. There is a decreasing tendency to be concerned about the doctrines and teaching of the church, while the emphasis on entertainment is accelerated. There is a steady and gradual erosion away from the historic teachings of the sundry denominations and an alarming decrease in biblical literacy. There is also an exorbitant amount of church shopping and an alarming decline in denominational loyalty. Worshipers become Sunday morning consumers who are shopping for the most delightful fare at the lowest price. Families that had once grown up in a denominational setting with a decidedly doctrinal stance are leaving at the slightest provocation and embracing ecumenism, Arminianism, Pentecostalism, and New Age cults.

This shift hit home recently while I was making a hospital call on a widowed octogenarian. During my visit, in walked an attractive, middle-aged niece of this dear saint, complete with an obviously Dutch name and roots in South Holland, a bastion of Calvinism if there ever was one. When I inquired about family connections and church affiliation, I was surprised to hear her proudly proclaim membership in a large church of another denomination. Adult-only baptism, Arminian theology, altar calls, and a practiced disdain for Calvinistic doctrine had apparently been exchanged for the faith in which she and her husband had been reared. Their children, too, all six of them, were now ex-Calvinists.

I suspect that the niece's Arminian church was rather excited to see and embrace these escaped Calvinists, but they can find little long-range comfort, for the stream runs in all directions. In many churches, the exit out the back door is wider than the entrance at the front. With no doctrinal discernment or depth of theological conviction, the sheep wander wherever the grass appears to be greenest.

Some of this theological shifting may have come about with the best of intentions. This lady expressed an unwillingness to put up with "all the theological quarreling" she had heard in her recent church home. Why could not people just love God and love their neighbors? Why could they not be about "the only business that really mattered," the bringing of lost souls to the Savior? Such arguments seem pious on the surface, but they betray a serious misunderstanding of the biblical message. Such folks have reduced the faith to an overly simplistic creed: "Love God and your neighbor too." Granted that these two commands are the summary of God's law, but such superficiality will not long endure in the heat of Satan's attacks and should be replaced with the whole armor of God.

Those who are unwilling to fight for truth, who are unwilling to put on the whole armor of God (Eph. 6:10–20), who want nothing but a life of joy and ease, had better wake up to the realities of this world. They had better learn that the Christian life is more complex than bringing people to a point of conversion, that the Great Commission is not the sum total of the biblical message, and that sanctification is the long and laborious process of living out the demands of our Lord and King. They better learn, too, that the devil "walks about like a roaring lion, seeking whom he may devour" (1 Peter 5:8). It would be wonderful if everyone on earth loved God and loved their neighbor as much as they loved themselves. But to think that such will occur in this life is naïveté of the worst sort. To experience such conditions we will have to find some way to get back into the Garden of Eden or wait until God calls us home to glory.

In this life we will have to fight. Each of us will have to choose the place where we want to stand and then be equipped with the best armor that can be had. We will do well to remind each other that "we do not wrestle against flesh and blood, but against . . . spiritual hosts of wickedness in the heavenly places" (Eph. 6:12). Our warfare is not against our brothers and our sisters but against the beliefs, the doctrines, and the worldviews that they espouse. In competition with the truths of God's Word are some potent belief systems that control and direct other people's lives.

Such belief systems as naturalistic evolution are relatively easy to spot and comparatively simple to combat, but Satan doesn't always present them in their stark, simplistic, indefensible forms. He comes instead with the subtleties of social Darwinism and theistic evolution, allowing plenty of room for God but reducing Him to an impotent, grandfather figure who is benignly admired in case we should get called to His home.

The devil also engages in subtle substitution. One of the most powerful disguises is that employed by the advocates of democracy. Already in his *Republic*, Plato knew instinctively that there was a chasm of difference between a republic and a democracy. In book 8 he says the democracy comes into being when "undisciplined young men, . . . in love with revolution, . . . luxurious and lazy in matters concerning both body and soul, . . . are careless of all else but making money."[5] When democracy is established, as it had been in his beloved Athens, "the city is full of freedom and liberty of speech, and men in it may do what they like. Where there is liberty of action, it is clear that each man would arrange his own private life in it just as it pleased him."[6]

In the culture of the West at the close of the second millennium A.D., most people have forgotten the difference between a republic and a democracy, thinking that the two are synonyms. When democracy is criticized, people bristle in anger and accuse the speaker of being unpatriotic, dictatorial, and antigovernment. Such was the case when Socrates and Plato condemned the democratic spirit that had pervaded Athens. In their estimation, democracy was the antithesis of the republic and bred a wholesale contempt of law, order, and civil behavior. When people claim that all men are equal in authority and that all power originates and resides with them, then the eternal truths of God's Word get trampled in the dirt. When men refuse to bow the knee to anyone, then no one is being submissive to Christ the King, who rules forever and forever.

The ways that the democratic gospel invades the church and the home and the school are beyond enumeration. The ways that feminists insist that women have the same privileges and rights as do men is one manifestation of the democratization of the church. The ways that gay and lesbian activists push their demands for full acceptance and even special privilege is another. The ways that those who are intellectually lazy push their demands for entertainment in the sanctuary is still another.

To be a Christian is to bow before the Lord and Master who has bought us with His blood. It is to recognize that He is, always has been, and always will be King of the universe. He didn't become King when He ascended into heaven and sat at the right hand of His Father (Luke 24:46–52; Acts 1:9–11). He already had been "Commander of the army of the LORD" since ancient times (Josh. 5:14).

We have been reminded that we are called to take every thought captive to Jesus Christ, to present it to Him, as a young child will do to his father or mother. Just as young children need to be reminded and warned that they live in a potentially hostile world where they may not accept rides with strangers, so we, as adults, are given similar warnings. We are not to hitch our hearts to nice-sounding phrases, to sweet-smelling words, unless we know the freight that they carry. Democracy may sound sweet and noble, full of toleration for all those neighbors we are supposed to love, but it thrives and grows on a deep-seated animosity toward all kingships, toward all who claim to be kings, Christ included.

During the 1840s, out of the state education office in Massachusetts, Horace Mann waged a ten-year campaign for common schools. Superintendent Mann thought it tragic that state moneys should be spent on schools operated by different denominations, when the religious differences among them seemed minor. Since the real business of the schools was to teach academic skills, he argued, why could not these religious communities consolidate their efforts, become more efficient, and form common or public schools? All that would be required would be to tone down or eliminate instruction about such fine points of doctrine as predestination, election, double determinism, sovereign grace, and infant baptism. These doctrines could be covered by the church on Saturday afternoon or Sunday morning. There was no need for causing controversy among Congregationalists, Presbyterians, Baptists, and Methodists. All that was needed was a shifting of responsibility for the propagation of divisive doctrine from the school to the church.[7]

The same argument is at work today in our colleges, our secondary schools, and our elementary institutions. With schools having opened their doors to people of every religious persuasion, the danger of offending those same new tuition payers and driving them back out the door has become very real. When schools have gone so far as to invite non-Christians into a Christian school, the risk becomes even greater. Not giving in to their demands opens the institution to charges of discrimination, a charge almost as explosive as "censorship" or "intolerance."

What is needed in our schools is a willing and open effort to inform students about the religious perspectives they will encounter if and when they enroll. To pretend to be wholly Christian when the truth is that they will be only partially Christian is deception of the worst sort. To pretend to be Roman Catholic, when most of the faculty are committed to secularism, is another brand of dishonesty. This subterfuge occurs across the spectrum, but it ought not to occur anywhere.

Those who claim to be Reformed should make that claim forthrightly and pointedly when they are recruiting students. Those who want to be Lutherans or Catholics or Baptists or Methodists should do the same, making their appeal not to their traditions or to the writings of their heroes but to the pages of God's Holy Word. Let all who claim to be Christian make their appeal to Jesus Christ, whose name they bear and whose Word they proclaim. If, under examination, their appeal cannot be sustained, let them modify it according to His eternal standard. His is the court of final appeal.

Curricular Warfare

During the early stages of American educational history, especially during the colonial era, there was little controversy about the make-up of the school curriculum. Basic skills such as writing, reading, and arithmetic were taught in essentially the same way, whether one was in Massachusetts, New York, or Georgia. There was a common religious commitment, too, with the Bible and the Westminster Catechisms serving as primary sources for teaching spiritual values. The New England primer and Noah Webster's speller served as the most widely accepted tools for instruction, with moral and religious truths bathing each lesson. At the secondary and university levels, there was a strong concentration of Greek and Latin, along with logic, mathematics, and theology, for the primary purpose of training men for the ministry.

As one compares that era with the world in which we live, it is obvious that the time of harmony is past and that our schools have become battlegrounds where ideologies of sundry stripes are striving for dominance. Throughout the nineteenth century, as the religious influence of the Puritans began to wane, it became apparent that there was intense competition in the academic marketplace. Practical skills such as surveying and bookkeeping, along with nature studies, began to push out theology and philosophy as staples. In the twentieth century new fields of study began to emerge, bearing such names as science, psychology, sociology, and anthropology. At the secondary level, the emphasis shifted from the academic and intellectual to the practical and vocational. As the society became more and more secular, denominations began to build more and more academies and colleges, spread across the land, in order to preserve the religious heritage they had taken with them from Europe. Presbyterians, Baptists, Lutherans, Congregationalists, Episcopalians, Methodists, Calvinists, and Mennonites of every stripe organized colleges to pass on the truths that they held dear. Each group could experience a measure of security within its enclave and ignore the rest, all the while bemoaning the state universities' expanding range of influence.

In our time, curriculum conflict seems to be almost continuous. With almost no one holding fast to the focus of a God-centered education but almost everyone supporting either the child-centered or the subject-centered approach, debate is constant. If one loves fights and debates, he has only to wait a few years and another one will break out. Some of those wars are repetitive and circular. Among those are the debates between vocational subjects and general education. At the elementary level, a perennial skirmish occurs between the advocates of phonetic and sight-sound reading approaches. At every level there is the conflict between African-American studies and conventional history. At the college and university levels, there is the debate between classical English and street stories, between traditional history and women's studies. In the field of teacher training there is the debate between the tabula rasa model and that of innate knowledge.

One debate that can serve us as example is that involving outcomes-based education (OBE), a debate that swirled across America through the middle 1990s. If one wanted to start a lively debate that might quickly get out of control, all one would have to do would be to mention OBE. In countless communities the clash of opinions on that issue was loud and long. In some of those communities, community itself was threatened. Tensions and feelings ran at fever pitch, with the opponents calling as their witnesses such conservative icons as Rush Limbaugh, Phyllis Schlafly, James Dobson, Cal Thomas, and a host of others. Epithets were hurled and name calling sometimes reached the level of practiced art.

James Dobson has been a courageous and powerful spokesman for the Christian community during some of our national debates. He has served admirably on commissions studying the effects of pornography and homosexuality. For his unabashed commitment to biblical values he has taken some tremendous criticism and has suffered persecution at the hands of our national media. I have long had a profound respect and admiration for Dobson and his Focus on the Family organization, but it was difficult to sympathize with him on the OBE issue. He and his staff intuitively recognized that there was something fundamentally amiss with OBE, but their critique missed the mark badly and served only to reinforce the efforts of those opposed to them. As so often happens, these arguments shed more heat than light.

In a feature article in the *Citizen,* Jeff Hooten observed correctly that "OBE emphasizes 'outcomes'—skills that all students must demonstrate—instead of traditional facts, figures and required courses."[8] Hooten goes on to suggest what he sees as a critical, evaluative question: "Is the outcome one that defines something we would expect a young person to do academically? Does it have something to do with arithmetic, science, English, history, geography or fine arts?" Presumably, if the answer is yes, the program is safe and worthy of support. He then insists that we ask the "opposite question" of OBE advocates and programs: "Does it have something to do with values, attitudes, or social outcomes that require certain behavior?" Presumably, if the answer is yes, the program is worthy of condemnation.

The article concludes: "Outcomes that talk about attitudes, values and feelings are wandering from the primary responsibility of the school, which is to make sure that kids know how to read, to write, to calculate."[9] The Focus on the Family organization has opted for traditional, subject-centered educational philosophy and demonstrates a serious misunderstanding of what Christian schools ought to be doing. Dobson may be an outstanding Christian spokesman on moral concerns, but he needs to reconsider his educational philosophy.

To divorce attitudes, values, and feelings from the process of schooling and to focus only on academic, subject-centered activities is to adopt a historic model of secular, public humanistic education that has been as morally and spiritually bankrupt as is the OBE model.

During the spring of 1994 this tension-filled debate settled into the school communities of the Grand Rapids, Michigan, Christian School Association and the Chicago Southwest Christian School Association. Many other Christian and public schools also debated the issue, raising the OBE acronym to the level of a national firestorm. Administrators and boards became engulfed in impassioned argument, drawing tremendous criticism from angry parents, pastors, and politicians. Students often jumped into the fray on the side of their parents, grabbing any excuse to attack the system that was trying to mold and shape them.

In a 1995 conference on Christian education, designed at least in part to address this issue, some of the speakers did an admirable and courageous job of trying to bring clarity out of chaos. One speaker began by wisely asserting the "OBE has been the source of mass confusion in the world of education, both secular and Christian. Thinking about outcomes," he asserted, "has created terrible tension."[10] With that assessment, no one would disagree.

For all who have read to this point and have studied "Which Learning Is Most Valuable" and "Which Learning Is Most Painful," or those who may have read my *Education in the Truth*, it will be apparent that one cannot avoid discussion of outcomes. Even though I have chosen not to use the word *outcomes* because of its potential for confusion, its synonyms (objectives, goals, aims, ends, or purposes) are liberally sprinkled throughout my pages. To not be concerned about the effects of all our planned educational activities on the lives of our students is folly of the highest sort. To insist, on the contrary, that we have a clear statement of what we are trying to accomplish or what it is that we are trying to teach to the children entrusted to our care is to make perfectly good and logical sense. We need to know clearly and precisely what we hope to achieve before we devise plans or methodologies for achieving that. To use an analogy from travel, we need to know where we want to go before we can decide on the best mode of transportation for getting there. If we merely want to walk to the corner store, there is no point in chartering an airplane or contracting for a cruise liner.

So, too, in education. If we determine that we must teach our children to drive a car, there is little point in building a swimming pool as a means to that end. If we want to teach them to discern between truth and falsehood, there is not much point in boring them with flash cards. If we want to teach them to obey authority, there is not much point in letting them choose their own curriculum. The objective or goal always determines, or ought to determine, the methodology to be employed. On the basis of one's chosen outcomes the educator must select the methods to be employed and the means by which to measure the degree of success in reaching those outcomes. Teaching methodologies and testing mechanisms must always follow after, and never precede, the selection of objectives or goals.

If we want to be fair to the proponents of OBE, to engage them in dialogue without offending them in any way, we might want to grant them their point. We could then point with a real measure of agreement to what Ralph W. Tyler preached in *Basic Principles of Curriculum and Instruction* (1949) and what Benjamin Bloom argued during the 1960s. We could also express a degree of consent with the competency-based education movement of the 1970s.

To express a measure of agreement, however, is not the same as buying into something. I can find points of agreement with the OBE movement, but I cannot and will not buy into it. Adopting the OBE system will create serious problems for any Christian. No administrator, no teacher, no board member, and no parent should adopt OBE as their program or even try to modify its philosophy. Let me explain why.

The primary argument against OBE is that it is thoroughly humanistic and is not in the least way Christian. Allow me to illustrate from the list of exit outcomes cited in the strategic plan of the Grand Rapids Christian School Association.[11] Since this was distributed to all the conferees at the Christian Schools International (CSI) convention in 1994, this has become public information and was defended by those who brought it. Their list of exit outcomes is given here in abbreviated form:

We know that we have accomplished our mission when students are:

(1) *collaborative workers* who demonstrate interpersonal skills and work toward common goals;
(2) *community contributors*, who contribute their time, energies, and talents to improving the welfare of others and the quality of life in their diverse communities;
(3) *discerning problem solvers*, who carefully identify and analyze problems; demonstrate creative thinking in the problem solving process; and examine solutions in light of God's word;
(4) *effective communicators* who are able to use and evaluate information and media;
(5) *complex thinkers* who identify, access, integrate, and use available resources and information to reason, make decisions, and solve complex problems in a variety of contexts;
(6) *quality producers* who create intellectual, artistic, and practical products, use tools and technology effectively, and demonstrate personal management skills.

Initial reactions to this list in most quarters would probably be quite favorable, even though the jargon is a bit thick for all those who are not in the inner circle of planners. Given explanation, one would be apt to express some guarded agreement with these exit outcomes, asserting that such qualities ought to characterize those who graduate from our secondary schools.

But more careful analysis should raise some fundamental questions. Is there anything distinctively Christian about this list? Is this a list that would set a Christian school apart from the public school down the street or from the private secular academy run for the elite? Only in the third point is there a hint of biblical values ("examine solutions in the light of God's word"). Given the paucity of biblical directives and the ambiguity of even this qualifier, it is not unfair to criticize this list as being little different from what one could expect from the state's bureaucratic policy makers.

But there are two even more pressing questions that must be raised. First, from what source or by what means did you derive this list? From where did these exit outcomes come? When the question was raised at the convention, the reply was that the school association had conducted a survey of teachers, parents, board members, and students, questioning them as to what they thought that students should accomplish while in their school system. From a vast array of responses, they did some number crunching and came out with a list of most often expressed outcomes. Assuming that they conducted the process fairly and designed the questionnaires with clarity, we could applaud them for being democratic. By common consent, they thought they had put the tension behind them.

In the process, however, a second, more fundamental question had not been asked. Given the assumption that these were Christian kids who had come from Christian homes, whose parents and teachers still believe those marvelous words of the first question and answer of the Heidelberg Catechism, had anyone consulted the One to whom those kids belong? Had anyone asked the Creator of the universe, the Redeemer of the elect, what He would like His children to learn? Had anyone consulted the God of the Bible to see if He had articulated there some goals or objectives or outcomes or standards for the Christian life? Was the Word of God still a sufficient guide for all of faith and life? Or has it been superseded by human opinion? Does God limit education to academic, subject-centered outcomes? Is God a traditionalist? Would God agree with Focus on the Family or with outcomes-based education? Or would He agree with neither?

The answer, I trust, is obvious. God is the source of all knowledge, and so knowledge is important. But "though I have the gift of prophecy, and understand all mysteries and all knowledge, . . . but have not love, I am nothing" (1 Cor. 13:2). If we do not "put to death . . . fornication, uncleanness, passion, evil desire, and covetousness, which is idolatry" (Col. 3:5), then all the knowledge and skills in the world will not keep us from the wrath of a holy and righteous God. If we do not design all of our programs in such a way that they strengthen the faith of our kids in their Creator and in His Holy Word, we have missed the mark. If we do not strive to teach them basic beliefs that will forever affect their behavior, we are no better than fools groping in the darkness.

But there is one other fundamental flaw in OBE that must be

noted. OBE claims to be outcome-based education. The clear message is that the entire program is based on outcomes or objectives. To make such a claim is either utmost naïveté about educational foundations or an act of flagrant deception. The proponents claim that the outcomes or goals are the foundation, or the basis, for the entire educational program, with nothing undergirding them. To make such a claim is to ignore or deceive the entire matter of anthropology, more simply articulated as statements and inferences about the nature of the child to be educated. In order to articulate some outcome or goal to be achieved, there must first be some existing condition or quality needing to be modified, refined, or corrected. To assert, for example, that a child must learn to read is to imply that in his existing state he does not yet know how to read. To assert, as God does, that a child must learn to honor his father and his mother is to imply that in his natural condition he does not willingly do so. To assert, as God does, that children must learn to obey authority is to imply that, by natural inclination, they are disobedient. There is always a presupposed condition or quality of the student that precedes any attempt to bring about any desired outcome. The OBE movement flagrantly ignored that most important dimension of educational philosophy. The OBE movement never consciously or openly asked What is the nature of the student that requires change and sanctification in his life? They never asked, "What is man that You are mindful of him?" (Ps. 8:4), as does the psalmist.

Christian educators should never ignore the matter of values, attitudes, emotions, or behaviors. All of them are essential to the loving, holy, and blameless lives that our Lord demands of us (1 Thess. 3:11–13). Christian education also should never be tricked into claiming that the schooling process is based on outcomes, for that is a foundation that is as deceptive as the devil and as shaky as sand. We must be reminded that all education should be based on the Bible. God is the only Author(ity) who can speak with any finality about the selection of outcomes or goals for the kids He has entrusted to our care. His Word must be the basis for all our thinking about the entire realm of education. If we no longer use that Word as our foundation, any programs we try to design will soon crack and come tumbling down.

The OBE conflict is history. But its demise will not mean the end of debate. Disputes will continue to beset us, until Christ comes again. While we live in this world of wars and rumors of wars, we need to look to the sovereign God of the universe to find the light that will lead us out of darkness.

Conclusion

Coming Full Circle: Built on a Firm Foundation

In response to the senseless tragedy at Columbine High School and similar schoolhouse massacres, Senator Sam Brownback (R-Kans.) and Senator Daniel Patrick Moynihan (D-N.Y.) have led a well-intentioned effort to establish a Special Senate Committee on American Culture. It would be charged with determining who is responsible for the trashing of American culture. On first reflection, one might conclude that such is a noble effort to address our collective chaos. Citing such broad cultural indicators as illegal drug use, sexual promiscuity, out-of-wedlock births, abortion rates, divorce rates, teen suicide, child abuse, and the amount of time children spend in front of the television, the senators and numerous bipartisan supporters have hoped to create a committee that could quantify, analyze, and change the kinds of cultural malaise plaguing our society. Overtly the intent is not to correct the problems but to identify and publicize them.

Pointing potential fingers of accusation at our public schools, at the Hollywood entertainment industry, and at our major media conglomerates, the senators were asked how they might effect the necessary kinds of changes once the problems had been identified. In reply, Senator Brownback rightly explained, "The way we change is by the millions of individual changes that people make, and the more you converse about that, the more of those changes you see. The national conversation we've had over the last several years has begun to have some impact on things like abortion and welfare mothers. That's what

161

we are talking about: just raising the level of our national conversation."[1] Presumably, if we can get enough people talking about the need for change, that dialogue in itself will precipitate the changes that are needed.

Eloquent as these speeches have sounded, the solution to the evils of American society does not lie in the formation of still another layer of government bureaucracy. Our experiences with the war on drugs should have convinced us of that. No matter how many laws we pass to protect our children from the sale and distribution of illegal drugs and no matter how many drug enforcement agents we post on our southern borders, the conclusion is clear. We are losing the war. Heroin, cocaine, and marijuana continue to be sold on the streets and alleys of our cities, not only by inner-city residents but also by all levels of society. As long as there is a national appetite, there will be a national market. As long as there are buyers, there will be sellers. The solution to our national drug problem does not lie in sending more military equipment to the mountains of Columbia or more enforcement agents to the streets of Philadelphia. Those efforts and expenditures are necessary and worth continuing, but they will not provide the answer.

The same is true for the problem of crime and murder. For some, the way to diminish the number of murders and robberies that occupy so much of our national news is to attack the manufacturers of the guns used in those crimes. For mayors of large cities to file lawsuits against the factories that produce guns may be politically advantageous on election day, but that will not cure the crimes of our culture.

The same must be said of those state attorneys general who wage legal battles against the nation's tobacco companies. The problem does not originate in the gun. It does not originate in the coca leaves. It does not originate in the cigarette. The problem originates in the human heart.

What we have experienced in our Western culture is the death of responsibility and the substitution of a victim mentality. From the highest levels of government to the lowest levels of community life, there is a deep-seated conviction that we are not responsible for our own actions. Murderers are not responsible for shooting their victims. Thieves are not responsible for breaking and entering. Rapists are not responsible for attacking women. Embezzlers are not responsible for doctoring accounts and stealing huge sums of money. Gamblers are not responsible for their addictions. Homosexuals are not responsible for their unnatural urges. And husbands blame midlife crises for committing adultery. It is easy to look for excuses. That comes naturally whenever we fail. It is easy to point the finger of blame at someone other than ourselves. Kids do it whenever they are accused. We all do.

Schools are no exceptions, for they can always blame the agencies that fund those schools. Most schools that fail to meet the expected standards insist that that is because their institutions have been underfunded. "Give us more money and we will become better" is their plaintive plea. "Let us become bigger and then we will improve." Much of the educational establishment in the Western world has operated on that premise for decades. Schools in our inner cities, for example, perform so poorly because they are underfunded, understaffed, and forced to accept students from impoverished homes. The schools therefore are not at fault but are the helpless victims of political processes and environmental pressures.

The Coleman Report of 1996 has been called "the most controversial educational document of the twentieth century." It was mandated by a little noticed section of the Civil Rights Act of 1994, which directed the U.S. Commissioner of Education to "conduct a survey . . . concerning the lack of availability of equal educational opportunity for individuals by reason of race, color, religion, or national origins."[2] The law stipulated that the commissioner was to submit a report to the president and to the Congress within two years.

The survey was hastily conducted and the report efficiently assembled, but the Democratic administration that had pushed for its issuance quickly squelched its distribution. What Coleman and his colleagues found was that

> wide disparities in academic achievement could not be attributed to differences in the quality of the schools minority-group students attended. . . . They had expected to find gross inequities in the quality of the schools attended by minority group students . . . and they had assumed that these inequalities would explain the inequalities in academic achievement.

After all, this assumption had been the basis for federal poli-
cies and most other education programs. . . . Differences in
school quality were not very closely related to differences in
student achievement; the cause-and-effect relationship between low student achievement and inadequate educational
inputs that they expected to find simply did not materialize.
On the contrary, neither black nor white nor Mexican-American,
Puerto Rican, Indian American, or Oriental children from a
given socio-economic background did significantly better in
schools with high per-pupil expenditures, modern plants,
large libraries, up-to-date curricula, and the like than in
schools with low expenditures, outdated plants and curricula,
and small libraries.[3]

Committed to a deeply held assumption of Locke's tabula rasa, the
administration could not place the blame for failure on those responsible but needed to fix the blame in a place where it could offer the
solution of Great Society programs. The myth of inequality must be
preserved.

The Coleman report has been misinterpreted to mean that
schools have no effect on student achievement. That conclusion is a
serious error, for then environment would be of no consequence.
Then we might as well all live in a pigsty. What the report did high-
light is the primary causal factors affecting academic performance or
lack of it. What parents do and say to their children is of far greater
significance than all the external factors normally associated with
school success. Parents are still the child's most influential teachers,
for good or for evil.

But even that is not the most important causal factor. The
Trenchcoat Mafia in Littleton could not blame their parents for arm-
ing them with bombs and guns. Reggie and Sammy could not blame
their parents for loading their car with rotten eggs. The kids who
refuse to do their assignments cannot accuse their progenitors for
their stubborn inattention to duty. No, the problem lies in the individual heart.

Solomon reminds us: "Keep your heart with all diligence, for out
of it spring the issues of life" (Prov. 4:23). Jesus reinforces that princi-

ple when He says, "Out of the abundance of the heart the mouth speaks. A good man out of the good treasure of his heart brings forth good things, and an evil man out of the evil treasure brings forth evil things" (Matt. 12:34–35). Our Lord made that even more explicit at another time, when He said, "From within, out of the heart of men, proceed evil thoughts, adulteries, fornications, murders, thefts, covetousness, wickedness, deceit, licentiousness, an evil eye, blasphemy, pride, foolishness. All these evil things come from within and defile a man" (Mark 7:21–23).

The Jews of Ezekiel's day had a proverb that they loved to utter: "The fathers have eaten sour grapes, and the children's teeth are set on edge" (Ezek. 18:2). It was a simple way of blaming their fathers for their own misdeeds and their sorry lot in life. They were not responsible; their fathers were. How convenient!

God, however, was not fooled and was not amused. In righteous anger, He replied,

> As I live, . . . you shall no longer use this proverb in Israel.
>
> "Behold, all souls are Mine;
> The soul of the father
> As well as the soul of the son is Mine. . . ."
>
> The soul who sins shall die. The son shall not bear the guilt of the father, nor the father bear the guilt of the son. The righteousness of the righteous shall be upon himself, and the wickedness of the wicked shall be upon himself. (Ezek. 18:3–4, 20)

Many of the principles that undergird our pedagogical endeavors have been rooted in erroneous thinking. Much of what even Christian communities have attempted has been compromised with philosophies from the secular university. The power of earlier Christian thought has been dissipated. We have become a thoroughly secular society. We have become progressively pagan, progressively evil. If we are to effect any kind of significant change, we will have to engineer a new national dialogue, a new approach that is truly rooted in divine wisdom. We will have to find a new basis for public policy. If we are to improve the schools where we send the kids that God has entrusted to us, we will have to listen more carefully to that God who has created them. We will have to consult His Word. We will have to get back to the Bible.

There we will find a true understanding of human nature, the right reasons for choosing curricula, true assumptions rooted in reality, and the difference between truth and falsehood. There we will find the courage to confront.

—Appendix A Learning Defined as Change

In a survey of recent literature, I noted that many authors who are intent on describing human behavior and the learning process use the word *change* as a key component in their definitions, even while avoiding the concept of change as crucial to their definitions. Almost unavoidably, they use the word while ignoring the basic idea. Here is a sampling of quotations:

Eric Hoffer

"It is my impression that no one really likes the new. We are afraid of it. It is not only as Dostoyevsky put it that 'taking a new step, uttering a new word is what people fear most.' Even in slight things the experience of the new is rarely without some stirring of foreboding."[1]

"Men never philosophize or tinker more freely than when they know that their speculation or tinkling leads to no weighty results. We are more ready to try the untried when what we do is inconsequential."[2]

"We know that words cannot move mountains, but they can move the multitude; and men are more ready to fight and die for a word than for anything else. Words shape thought, stir feeling, and beget action; they kill and revive, corrupt and cure. The 'men of words'—priests, prophets, intellectuals—have played a more decisive role in history than military leaders, statesmen, and businessmen."[3]

B. R. Bugleski

"Learning is the process of the formation of relatively permanent neural circuits through the simultaneous activity of the elements of the circuits-to-be; such activity is of the nature of *change* in cell structures through growth in such a manner as to facilitate the arousal of the entire circuit."[4]

Lee Cronbach

"Learning is shown by a *change* in behavior as a result of experience."[5]

Robert M. W. Travers

"Learning is said to have occurred when a response undergoes modifications on its recurrence as a result of conditions in the environment which have produced relatively permanent *changes* in the central nervous system. It will be noted that the definition excludes *changes* in behavior due to fatigue or other local conditions."[6]

G. M. Blair, R. S. Jones, and R. H. Simpson

"What is learning? Any *change* of behavior which is a result of experience, and which causes people to face later situations differently may be called learning."[7]

Henry C. Lindgren

"Learning consists of the *changes* in behavior that result from interaction with the environment, and reinforcement is the basic event that makes learning possible."[8]

Neal Miller

"Learning is the process of achieving homeostasis or equilibrium; it is the process of overcoming *change* and returning to a stable condition."[9]

Edward L. Thorndike

"Learning is the mechanical process of stamping in neural connections or stimulus-response bonds."[10]

Edwin R. Guthrie

"Learning is habit formation."[11]

B. F. Skinner
"Learning is habit formation brought into existence by reinforcement."[12]

Edward C. Tolman
"Purposive behaviorism is concerned with the effort of external stimuli on behavior, i.e., with learning, with the way that behavior *changes* with *changing* experience of the external world."[13]

"Learning involves *changes* in cognitions resulting from experience with external stimuli."[14]

P. A. Howie and G. Winkleman
"We have already established that each child enters school with his own set of coping skills, based upon his own individual set of experiences. Now we must decide which coping patterns we will accept and develop, and which we should reject and *change*."[15]

George R. Knight
"For present purposes, learning may be defined as 'the process that produces the capability of exhibiting new or *changed* human behavior (or which increases the probability that new or *changed* behavior will be elicited by a relevant stimulus), provided that the new behavior or behavior *change* cannot be explained on the basis of some other process or experience'—such as aging or fatigue."[16]

Appendix B Christianity versus Democracy

CHRISTIANITY	DEMOCRACY
1. God alone is sovereign.	Man is sovereign.
2. Faith in God.	Faith in man.
3. Law abiding precedes law making.	Law making precedes law abiding.
4. Law originates with God.	Law originates with man.
5. Man's goals are obedience and freedom through Christ.	Man's goals are liberty and happiness.
6. The powers that be are ordained of God. Governors and presidents and kings are ministers of God.	Government is of, by, and for the people. Elected officials are the servants of the majority.
7. The voice of God is either proclaimed or perverted by the people.	The voice of the people is the voice of God.
8. Jesus is God's Son and King of the universe.	Jesus is the great democrat who preached the brotherhood of all men.

9. Man belongs to his faithful Savior.

Man belongs to himself and never to anyone else.

10. Man's end is predestined by God.

Man is the master of his own fate.

11. Man bows in subjection to Christ as Lord.

Man bows the knee to no one.

12. Heaven in eternity is promised to believers.

Heaven on earth can be achieved by man.

"Let every soul be subject to the governing authorities. For there is no authority except from God, and the authorities that exist are appointed by God. Therefore whoever resists the authority resists the ordinance of God, and those who resist will bring judgment on themselves. For rulers are not a terror to good works, but to evil. Do you want to be unafraid of authority? Do what is good, and you will have praise from the same." (Rom. 13:1–3)

"You are the final, ultimate judges of what is best for you. You are the ones to establish policy—no minority, no authority, no special-interest group—only you. Thus you must have faith not only in yourself but in your fellow citizens. If you possess this faith, you believe in democracy; if you do not possess it, you do not believe in democracy regardless of the words you use." (Theodore Brameld, *Education as Power* [New York: Holt, Rinehart and Winston, 1965], 37.)

Appendix C   Ten Rules for Effective Discipline

1. *Don't shout or scream.* Shouting or screaming indicates lack of control and becomes a public embarrassment that often results in retaliation and revenge. Children will want to get even.

2. *Respect every child.* Remember that every child is created in the image of God. If we expect them to respect us, we have to earn that respect. We teach best by modeling.

3. *Be consistent. Do not contradict others in authority.* If fathers and mothers do not agree, they must settle their differences privately and not confuse the child. The same holds for school administrators and teachers.

4. *Stop little things.* Do not wait for a major act of disobedience, but respond in scale to small demonstrations of defiance or resistance. A pause, a look, or a stare will usually stop problems before they become large.

5. *Insist on rules of courtesy.* When one person is speaking, all the rest should be listening. Learning to listen is an underrated objective. It demonstrates a willingness to learn, a respect for others, and courtesy.

6. *Do not publicize offenses or punishment in front of others.* Offenders are not helped by public embarrassment, just as they are not helped by screaming. Public embarrassment encourages public retaliation.

7. *Do not make idle threats.* Too many parents and teachers try to control behavior by making threats that they either cannot or will not carry out. Students will soon recognize these threats as hollow and ignore them.

8. *Be certain that punishment hurts but does not injure.* If punishment does not hurt, it is not punishment. If it causes injury, then it should be forbidden. Staying indoors for recess is not punishment on a cold, rainy day. Spanking is not punishment if the one being spanked laughs through its administration.

9. *Use punishment appropriate to the age.* Corporal punishment (spanking) is necessary at younger ages because understanding is not yet mature. Withholding automobile or dating privileges will be more effective with sixteen-year-olds.

10. *Remember that teaching is the primary meaning and purpose of all discipline.* Punishment is applied only after steps 1, 2, and 3 of the definition of discipline (pp. 131–32) have failed. When you are discouraged with results, consult the dictionary again and pray for both patience and perseverance.

Notes

Introduction

1 Joel Belz, *World*, May 22, 1999, 7.
2 Statistical Abstract of the United States, 1999 ed., reported in *USA Today*, December 14, 1999, 1A.

Chapter 1: Understanding the Dilemma

1 Cal Thomas, "Educating Children vs. Preserving an Institution," *The Outlook*, May 1999, 14.
2 Lest the reader be surprised and offended by this quotation from God, please remember that our culture has radically confused jealousy with envy. Envy is always wrong, but jealousy is a virtue because it is an attribute of God. Even the New International Version participates in this confusion and lists jealousy as a sin, when the sin that should be listed is envy. Jealousy is a deep-seated desire to protect and preserve those who are loved and belong to that person. A man rightly is jealous for his wife but wrongly envies his neighbor because of his wife.

Chapter 2: Do We Dare Talk Philosophy?

1 I will occasionally, for the sake of simplicity, use male pronouns to refer to both genders. The reader should not infer from this any bias against women.
2 Ralph W. Tyler, *Basic Principles of Curriculum and Instruction* (Chicago: University of Chicago Press, 1949).
3 Ibid., 1.
4 Norman De Jong, *Education in the Truth* (Nutley, N.J.: Presbyterian and Reformed, 1969).
5 For the most insightful and comprehensive analysis of Van Til's apologetic system, see Greg L. Bahnsen, *Van Til's Apologetic: Readings and Analysis* (Phillipsburg, N.J.: Presbyterian and Reformed, 1998).

6 John Dewey, "My Pedagogic Creed," in *Three Thousand Years of Educational Wisdom*, ed. Robert Ulich (Cambridge, Mass.: Harvard University Press, 1963), 629.

7 See chapter 3 for an analysis of this false god.

8 The reader is referred to Norman De Jong, *Education in the Truth* (Nutley, N.J.: Presbyterian and Reformed, 1969), chap. 1, for a discussion of the relation between faith and reason. The rationalist puts faith in reason (i.e., deductive logic) rather than in the revelation of the triune God.

Chapter 3: How Do We Find Answers?

1 See the section "Who Are Scientists?" for an analysis of science and how it is to be understood.

2 Josh McDowell, "Truth and Tolerance," *Focus on the Family*, August 1999, 6.

3 George M. Marsden, *The Soul of the American University* (New York: Oxford University Press, 1994), 382.

4 Charles Hodge, *What Is Darwinism?* (New York: Scribner, Armstrong and Co., 1874), 126.

5 David C. Lindberg, and Ronald L. Numbers, "Beyond War and Peace: A Reappraisal of the Encounter Between Christianity and Science," unpublished paper, 1986.

6 Charles Lyell, *Principles of Geology* (1839; reprint, Hafner Service, 1970), 1:164.

7 Stephen Gould, "Evolution and the Triumph of Homology, or Why History Matters," *American Scientist*, January–February, 1986, 61.

8 Eric Hoffer, *The True Believer* (New York: Harper and Row, 1958), 18.

Chapter 4: How Should We Understand Kids?

1 Plato *Phaedo* 80b. The numbers in the footnotes are the page numbers of the Stephanus edition of Plato's works.

2 Ibid. Note that Plato asserts a body-soul dichotomy, which creates all sorts of religious-philosophic problems for Christians. It is not our purpose to refute or debate these issues in this context.

3 Note that Plato speaks always of a Good and not of God. Plato is not a Christian and not even a monotheist. Many Christians have failed to recognize that.

4 Plato *Phaedo* 75b–75d.

5 Ibid., 65c and 66.

6 The male pronoun is used as a reflection of Greek thought, which gave no place to the education of girls or women.

7 Plato *Phaedo* 73 and 76.

8 Aristotle *Nicomachean Ethics*, quoted in *Three Thousand Years of Educational Wisdom*, ed. Robert Ulich (Cambridge, Mass.: Harvard University Press, 1963), 78.

9 John Locke, "Essay Concerning Human Understanding," contained in *Fundamentals of Philosophy*, ed. Errol Harris (New York: Holt, Rinehart and Winston, 1969), 226–27.

10 This section originally appeared, slightly modified, in *The Outlook*, January 1991, 11–13.

Chapter 5: How Corrupt Are We?

1 New Geneva Study Bible, 1767.

Chapter 6: What Must I Become?

1 John R. W. Stott, *Christ the Controversialist* (Downers Grove, Ill.: InterVarsity Press, 1970).

Chapter 7: What Must the Child Learn?

1 Robert Ulich, *Education in Western Culture* (New York: Harcourt, Brace and World, 1965), 127.

2 Consult the section "Curriculum Warfare" in chapter 10 for a sample of that confusion.

3 Nicholas Wolterstorff, *Educating for Responsible Action* (Grand Rapids: Eerdmans, 1980), 3–4.

4 Jay E. Adams, "The Need for Inner Change," in *How to Help People Change* (Grand Rapids: Zondervan, 1986), 3–4.

5 Westminster Media Catalog, Westminster Theological Seminary, Philadelphia, Pennsylvania. Call 1-800-WRS-TAPE.

6 Gene Edward Veith, "Hollywood Goes Spiritual. Why should the devil get all the good movies?" *World*, October 2, 1999.

7 Augustine, *The Confessions* (New York: Pocket Books, Cardinal ed., 1952), 9–11.

Chapter 8: Who Is Responsible for Educating?

1 The Oregon Case, 1925 (268 U.S. 510). The original law, passed in 1922, was advocated by the Ku Klux Klan, which had argued that all private and parochial schools, especially those initiated by Roman Catholics, should be abolished, and that all children should be required to attend public schools.

2 For an excellent summary of those battles, see Laurie Vanden Heuvel, "Homeschooling: An Educational Choice," *The Outlook*, September 1996, 4–7.

3 The NEA and the AFT are both militant unions representing public school faculty. They have been irrevocably opposed to any tax support going to other than public schools.

Chapter 9: Implementing the Program

1 Credit for this title goes to Dr. James Dobson, whose excellent book by this same name has been a boon to millions of parents.
2 It is always prudent for teachers to report discipline cases to parents before the offenders get opportunity to tell their version of the story. In the case of traditional schools, it is wise for teachers to place a quick phone call to one of the parents before the car pool arrives or the bus drops off the youngster at home. Students don't always tell the truth when they have opportunity to give first report.
3 "Doctors group calls spanking bad medicine," *Chicago Tribune*, April 7, 1998, sect. 1, 6. The article was quoting from the group's magazine, *Pediatrics*.
4 "Ritalin Use Rising Sharply," *Chicago Tribune*, February 29, 1996, sect. 1, 19.
5 Herman Bavinck, *The Doctrine of God* (Edinburgh: Banner of Truth, 1979), 15.
6 William Barclay, *Letters* (Philadelphia: Westminster Press, 1975), 238.

Chapter 10: Who Will Teach Reformed Doctrine?

1 "Disharmony on Campus," *Grand Rapids Press*, May 1, 1999, sect. B, 1.
2 Ibid.
3 Ibid., 3.
4 The reader is encouraged to read my dissertation, "Boyd H. Bode, A Study of the Relationship Between the Kingdom of God and Democracy," available from University of Michigan Microfilms, Ann Arbor, Michigan. See also my *Christianity versus Democracy* (Nutley, N.J.: Craig Press, 1977).
5 Plato *Republic* 555–56.
6 Ibid., 557.
7 This was especially appealing to Mann, who was a staunch Unitarian and who found the teachings about the Trinity to be divisive and best left to the churches. The net effect was that Jesus Christ was pushed out of His own schools and replaced by a monotheistic deity called God.
8 Jeff Hooten, *Citizen*, August 21, 1995, 2.
9 Ibid., 4.
10 David Koetje, superintendent of the Grand Rapids Christian schools, Grand Rapids, Michigan. Notes taken by the author.
11 Working draft, Grand Rapids Christian Schools Association, January 1994.

Conclusion

1 Bob Jones, "Congress' Culture Cops," *World*, October 2, 1999.
2 Charles Silberman, *Crisis in the Classroom* (New York: Random House, 1970), 71. For a thorough analysis of this controversial but significant study, read 62–79. See also Christopher Jencks, "A Reappraisal of the Most Controversial Educational Document of Our Time," *New York Times Magazine*, August 10, 1969.
3 Silberman, *Crisis in the Classroom*, 71.

Appendix A: Learning Defined as Change

1 *The Ordeal of Change* (New York: Harper and Row, Perennial ed., 1963), 3.
2 Ibid., 91.
3 Ibid., 106.
4 *The Psychology of Learning* (New York: Holt, 1956), 5.
5 *Educational Psychology*, 2nd ed. (New York: Harcourt, Brace and World, 1963), 71.
6 *Essentials of Learning* (New York: Macmillan, 1963), 29.
7 *Educational Psychology* (New York: Macmillan, 1954), 93.
8 *Educational Psychology in the Classroom*, 3rd ed. (New York: John Wiley and Sons, 1967), 39.
9 In Winfred F. Hill, *Learning: A Survey of Psychological Interpretations*, 3d ed. (New York: Harper and Row, n.d.), 56.
10 In ibid., 54–56.
11 In ibid., 38.
12 In ibid., 81.
13 In ibid., 135.
14 In ibid., 137.
15 *Behavior Modification: A Practical Guide for the Classroom Teacher* (West Nyack, N.Y: Parker, 1977), 44.
16 *Philosophy and Education: An Introduction in Christian Perspective*, 2d ed. (Berrien Springs, Mich.: Andrews University Press, 1989), 10.

Index